Marriage at Its Best

John Allan Lavender

ACCENT BOOKS

Denver, Colorado

Except where otherwise indicated, Scripture quotations are from the *New American Standard Bible,* copyright © THE LOCKMAN FOUNDATION 1960, 1962, 1963, 1968, 1971, 1972, 1973, and are used by permission. Some verses are also quoted from *The Amplified Bible, The New Testament in Modern English,* by J. B. Phillips; and the *New International Version.*

ACCENT BOOKS

A division of Accent Publications, Inc.
12100 W. Sixth Avenue
P. O. Box 15337
Denver, Colorado 80215

Copyright ©1982 Accent Publications, Inc.
Printed in the United States of America

First published in 1978 with the title, *Your Marriage Needs Three Love Affairs*, this work has been updated and expanded to articulate God's "both/and" answer.

Library of Congress Catalog Card Number 82-71375

ISBN 0-89636-091-1

Second Printing

TO LUCILLE
my wife, my sweetheart
and my best friend!

By John Allan Lavender

- *Hey! There's Hope!*
- *Hang Tough in a Hostile World*
  —a study of the Book of Hebrews
- *Marriage At Its Best*

CONTENTS

By Way of Introduction

Given one how-to, you can solve one problem. Equipped with one principle, you can respond to a whole range of problems. This book brings you ten biblical principles, plus a generous sprinkling of practical suggestions throughout, to help you and your mate to make yours a *marriage at its best*.

There is a tremendous difference, however, between an acceptable marriage in the eyes of the world and the great marriage God wants for His children. Yet it takes more than the uniting of two Christians to achieve God's ideal marriage. It requires the mating of two *growing* Christians who resolutely refuse to settle for anything less than God's best.

Don't think, though, that we have overlooked God's concern for the Christian married to a non-Christian mate. Chapter Nine, presenting The Principle of Submission as Strategy, deals with this situation and applies equally well to those marriages involving carnal Christians.

Regardless of where you stand right now in your marriage, if both of you are willing to master and be mastered by the biblical principles for Christian marriage as given here, you will have the delightful experience of discovering what it means to be one flesh.

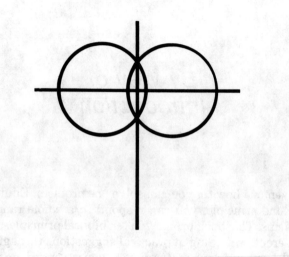

1

The Principle of Fullness
Before Overflow

Perfect marriage! Who on earth has one of those?

Julie, our youngest, put the question just that way. She and I had been discussing some of the principles presented in this book. "Do you and Mom have a perfect marriage?" she asked.

"Sometimes," I answered. "It all depends on whether we're both filled with the Holy Spirit or are controlled by our human spirit. When the latter is true, we have all kinds of trouble, as you well know!"

Julie grinned and nodded vigorously. For better or worse, our kids have seen us both better and worse!

"But," I continued, "when Mom and I each deliberately choose to be controlled by the Holy Spirit (which is what being filled with the Spirit means), then we really do have a perfect marriage and it's wonderful."

"You bet!" Julie exclaimed.

As I have attempted to teach all three of our children, perfect marriage is not a static state. It is an ever-growing and maturing relationship between two Spirit-filled Christians who are unwilling to settle for anything less than God's best. The one certain source of dependable instruction regarding that kind of exciting marriage is God's written word. The landmark passage with which one must begin consists of the first three chapters of Genesis.

Here, at the outset of scripture, God addresses Himself to this subject, establishing the fact that from His perspective a good marriage is not optional, it is foundational. It is the bedrock upon which every other relationship is built.

In the graphic that appears at the front of this book the two wedding rings overlap. This symbolizes the important truth that, while as partners in a Christian marriage you and your mate both retain a sphere of private interests, there is an overlapping area representing your paired interests—your marriage.

The relationship between these spheres of marriage—your private and paired interests—is not static, but constantly changing. During moments of intense mutual focus upon some shared interest, the level of closeness may be so high as to be symbolized by rings which virtually merge. At other times the demands of a private interest may be reflected in rings which overlap only part way. But—and here's the most important part—the intersecting cross suggests that if the two of you learn to obey Christ in the area of your paired interests, your private interests will be much more satisfying and secure. Conversely, if you fail in the area of your shared interests, your private interests will be seriously impaired.

When things aren't right at home, it is excruciatingly difficult to keep things right in other spheres. In fact, if things aren't right at home, they probably won't really be right in any area of life. Therefore, it's imperative that you see what God intends your marriage to be. The place to discover that is in scripture.

God above Everything

When you read the opening lines of Genesis, you find God dwelling in solitary splendor. The Unbegun Beginning. The Uncaused Cause. The Uncreated Creator.

A precocious six-year-old slipped into the nursery one day, tiptoed to the crib holding his newborn brother and peeked through the slats at this "little bundle from heaven," as his parents called the baby. He whispered,

"Tell me about God before you forget."

Fortunately, God does that for us. He tells us about Himself through creation—His statement in space. Through Jesus—His statement in human flesh. Through scripture—His statement in language. Among the things He tells us about Himself in Holy Writ is that He acted to bring the world into being.

He explains how bit by bit, piece by piece, object by object, He initiated and instigated everything that is. Everything comes from Him. Everything looks to Him. Everything is held together by Him. He is creator and sustainer of it all. Therefore, life as it was meant to be—life at its best—begins with God above everything. With God above everything, anything is possible.

As you move on through the first two chapters of Genesis, you discover Adam happy, busy, contented and fulfilled. Dwelling with God as he does, in a close, open-hearted, loving relationship, Adam discovers God to be so vastly wonderful, so utterly and completely delightful, that He can, without anything other than Himself, meet Adam's deepest needs. Enthralled by the wonder of such intimacy, Adam listens intently as God lays down a few simple rules for his life upon earth, and explains how it is to be with him in his Edenic home.

As you survey the picture painted on the opening pages of scripture, the message comes through loud and clear: *When Adam is involved in a genuine loving relationship with God, he experiences a blessed state of self-realization. He is a whole person. The atmosphere in which he lives is restful, relaxed, and altogether beautiful.*

Then God says and does something extraordinary. But let's follow the sequence directly from scripture: "Then the Lord God said, 'It is not good for the man to be alone'" (Genesis 2:18). Notice, it wasn't *Adam* who said that. As far as we can tell from the biblical record, there is no evidence Adam expressed any lack. As far as he was concerned Adam enjoyed complete self-realization. The fullness of his relationship with God was enough.

But God looked at this man who was so happily fulfilled and said, "It isn't good that he should go on living alone, I'll make a partner for him." Or, as the scripture puts it, "a helper suitable for him" (2:18). "So the Lord God caused a deep sleep to fall upon the man, and he slept; then He took one of his ribs, and closed up the flesh at that place. And the Lord God fashioned into a woman the rib which He had taken from the man, and brought her to the man. And the man said, 'This is now bone of my bones, and flesh of my flesh'" (Genesis 2:21-23).

We don't have an adequate translation of the little word "this." It's an untranslatable Hebrew expletive akin to our English exclamation, "wow!" The Living Bible does a pretty good job of translating it when it has Adam say, "This is it!"

At any rate, you don't have to exercise much imagination to feel what Adam must have felt when he awoke, looked up, saw Eve, and said, " [Wow! This is it!] This is now [at last!] bone of my bones, and flesh of my flesh; she shall be called Woman, because she was taken out of Man.' For this cause a man shall leave his father and his mother, and shall cleave to his wife; and they shall become one flesh. And the man and his wife were both naked and were not ashamed" (Genesis 2:23-25). It occurs to me as I reflect on this passage that God's intention for you is that your marriage be such that you and your mate have no need to be ashamed.

It is obvious from scripture, then, that marriage was God's idea. It was God who said it is not good that man should be alone. It was God who knew of Adam's need for human companionship, comfort and conversation. Out of the fullness of a healthy relationship with God came the overflow of Eve. She was not an afterthought, because, living as He does in an Eternal Now, God is incapable of afterthoughts.

Eve was not afterthought. She was overflow! She was

12

the natural outcome of God's love for Adam.

When God gave her to the man, it was not His intention that Eve should take His place. Nor did He have any desire to take her place. She was to do for Adam what God could not do. And God was to retain His rightful place in each of their lives, doing for them what only He could do.

God in Everything

This leads us to a second insight. God is not only *above* everything, God is *in* everything. He is in the way things are made. He is in the way things are used. He is in the creation of the earth. He is in the tilling, keeping, dressing and replenishing of the earth. He is in the dynamic attraction between male and female. He is in the childlike fascination with which Adam and Eve so thoroughly enjoyed each other. He is in the concept of marriage and the home. God is in everything!

Everything? you ask. Even the fall about which we read in Chapter 3? Yes, even the fall.

To be sure, Satan was the instigator of that awful event, and his every intent was evil. So when I say God was in the fall, I don't mean to suggest it was His idea. What I do mean is that, by the time God had filtered Satan's evil intent through His love for Adam and Eve, it had become His permissive will for them. Something He permitted because it provided an opportunity for Him to teach poor, old, gullible Adam and sweet little Eve the single most important lesson two people can ever learn: Life will only work out one way—God's way!

There's a fable about Adam who one day was out walking with his sons, Cain and Abel. As they passed the Garden of Eden Cain asked, "Why don't we move into that lovely place, Dad?"

"We used to live there," Adam replied, "but your mother ate us out of house and home!"

That's only partly true, of course. Adam was culpable, too. But beyond the humor is the fact that God permitted the fall in order for both Adam and Eve—and their sons and their sons' sons—to learn that life will only work out one way: God's way.

Because those two primal parents did not put Him and His will first, God, who is above everything and in everything, set about using everything—including the fall—to teach them life's most important lesson. Thus, by the time it had been filtered through His love for them, the fall had become God's permissive will for them. It was clay in His hands as the Heavenly Father began to remold Adam and Eve into what they had previously been.

Fullness before Overflow

What does this exposition from Genesis have to do with making the most of your marriage? Plenty. *Marriage as God meant it to be presumes each partner will be involved in a uniquely personal, intimate, loving relationship with God Himself.* At the base of most marital difficulties is a failure by one or both of the partners to put God above everything. To become involved—and stay involved—with Him in a genuine, loving way.

Christian marriage is not only a union of two bodies. It is not even just a union of two souls; i.e., two sets of mind, emotions and will. Christian marriage is primarily a mating of two spirits. For that reason, there is no more serious letdown in married life than for you or your mate to fail to maintain a genuine loving relationship with God.

Someone has said marriage is a union which defies management. But that's wrong. It only requires the right management—the management of God who established The Principle of Fullness Before Overflow.

Occasionally someone will ask, "Am I free to marry?" I have come to realize that person is asking the wrong question. A much more basic concern should be, "Am I free *not* to marry? Am I free to remain single because I am letting God meet my deepest needs?"

Until a person is able to stand alone, he or she cannot effectively stand with another. If one tries it, his or her marriage will self-destruct. This is a principle everyone must learn or be in for trouble.

A young girl, for instance, must realize God alone can fill the cup of her deepest needs. A husband, if the Lord provides one for her, will merely be the overflow of that full cup. If she marries before a continuing experience of fullness, that is, before she has achieved true realization of her personhood in and through Christ, she will be creating all kinds of problems for herself. Marriage will not be overflow. It will be avalanche—uncontrolled bursts of destructive human effort to find in a man what can only be found in God.

And, of course, the same thing applies to her fiance. He, too, must honor The Principle of Fullness Before Overflow lest he become possessive. A psychic vampire who sucks the energy he needs for survival from those around him—especially the one closest to him.

A village preacher was walking to church one Sunday morning when he met a young chap going in the opposite direction. The preacher stopped him and said, "Good morning, friend. Do you ever attend a place of worship?" The young man replied with a smile, "Yes indeed, sir, regularly. I am on my way to see her now."

Well, it's nice to know he thought so highly of his girl, but the fact is he had it all wrong. We are to love each other. We are to worship God. If you get the relationships out of order—if you violate The Principle of Fullness Before Overflow—your marriage is in peril.

Perhaps you want to put God first, but your partner insists that he or she be first. Clearly that person does not understand what he or she is asking. To be first in another person's life is to say, "I want to be God to you. I am willing to be and do all the Godlike things you need."

Anyone who has ever tried that, has found it to be an intolerable burden. An utter and absolute impossibility. No human being is capable of meeting the deepest needs of another. Only God can do that.

It is equally destructive for you to ask your partner to be first in your life. Or to ask that you be first in your partner's life. Again, that is putting a person in the place of God and no human being can fill in for Him. To attempt it is to pre-program your marriage to failure. Inevitably, the idol and the idolator devour each other. The principle is fullness *before* overflow expressed in a readiness to put God above everything. To become involved—and stay involved—with *Him* in a genuine, loving way.

In authentic love your partner is not accepted as a god, but as a gift of God. As such, he or she is unique and irreplaceable. A sacred trust. And it's absolutely thrilling to consider the fact that in Christian marriage at its best—marriage based upon the mating of two persons who have sought fullness before overflow—each of you is God's gift to the other in order that you may minister to one another and become a means of His shaping both of you into the persons you are meant to be.

Exactly Right for Each Other

This brings me around to the second application I want to draw from our biblical exposition. The Principle of Fullness Before Overflow not only necessitates that you put God *above* everything in your marriage, but that you learn to see God *in* everything in your marriage.

God's purpose in giving Eve to Adam and Adam to Eve was for their mutual benefit. She was exactly right for him. He was precisely right for her. When they got their priorities mixed up and failed to put God above everything, the good Lord moved into their new circumstance to fulfill His original intention for them. They were still right for each other; only now, instead of working through their wholeness, God had to work through their brokenness, using each to help the other find healing again.

He has the same goal for you. Perfect marriage is not one in which there are not problems. It is a vital, growing, maturing relationship designed to bring healing to both partners because they have learned to see God in everything, especially in the problems and annoyances which spring from their fallen nature.

God wants you to experience His highest in order that you may become your best. To do this, He must deal with the residual effects of your Adamic nature. One of the most effective ways He has of doing this is to work through your marriage.

Now, I want to be clearly understood. I am not saying God is the instigator of all the irritations which occur in your home. I am saying, however, that if you are a born-again Christian, you have been sealed by the Holy Spirit so nothing can come to you without God's knowledge and consent. A particular annoyance may be bred by the weakness or wickedness of your mate, but, by the time God filters that irritation through His love for you, it becomes His permissive will for you. He allows it in order to motivate you to deal with those qualities and characteristics within you which are unbecoming to a Christian.

Because your marriage mate knows every flaw and blind spot in your nature, he or she is precisely right for you because he or she knows exactly what to do to bring out the worst in you, which God, in turn, filters through His love and uses to confront you with your need to grow.

The preceding paragraph may seem wacky to you, but it's absolutely key. If you can get hold of this principle, it will transform your attitude toward your marriage and your marriage mate. It will also change your attitude toward every other person with whom you come in contact, either in or outside your home. You will learn to see that, in the particular circumstance involving that other person, he or she is precisely right for you. Or to put it another way, he or she is exactly what the Great Physician ordered in order to make you whole.

Seeing God in everything gives you a whole new perspective toward life. It will help you be positive toward negatives. It will put hope in your present situation, in the circumstances and relationships which exist this very moment. It will put an end to murmuring and complaining against those who are closest to you. It will make you loving and patient with those who annoy and trouble you. Instead of cursing them you will learn to bless and praise God for them, because each annoyance will trigger the fervent prayer,

> "Lord, what are You trying to teach me through this irritation? What blind spot in me are You trying to bring to light? How do You want to change me by making me like Jesus through this annoyance?"

As you become proficient and *prompt* in praying that prayer, you will discover those things which you have resisted and resented in your mate are precisely those qualities and characteristics which God is using to motivate you to the point of action and growth. Therefore, they are the sweetest and best things which could happen to you.

That doesn't mean you will always enjoy the maturing process. As the Bible explains, "All discipline for the moment seems not to be joyful" (Hebrews 12:11). But, as you let God turn your irritations into the source of a full-cup relationship with Him, you will learn to praise Him for being in everything because His plan for you is better than any you could make for yourself.

Hannah Smith, to whom I am indebted for making this ancient biblical concept come to life again for me, personally, illustrates this truth in a beautiful way.[1] She writes of a mother giving medicine to her sick child. The bottle holds the medicine, but the mother gives it. The bottle, therefore, is not responsible, the mother is. Out of all the bottles in her medicine chest, she will not allow one drop to pass the lips of her child unless she believes it will help bring healing. On the other hand, if she is convinced the medicine will promote health, her very love for the child will compel her to force that little one to take the medicine no matter how bitter it may taste.

Continuing Hannah Smith's analogy, the people around you, especially those closest to you, are often the bottles that hold your medicine. But it is the Heavenly Father's hand of love which pours out the medicine and, if need be, compels you to take it.

That does not mean God is the instigator of all the distressing actions and attitudes which bug you in your marriage. These probably spring from sin in the soul of your mate. Therefore, the things themselves cannot be called God's will. But by the time the Heavenly Father filters these actions and attitudes through His love for you, they become His will for you, the very medicine you need to promote spiritual health and growth.

Should you resent the human bottle then, just because it holds the medicine you need? Of course not. Instead you should praise God for that person, because he or she is exactly right for you. And I might add, you are exactly right for him or her.

This word of caution: To say you are exactly right for your mate does not excuse carnality on your part. You miss the point completely if you respond to this concept with the attitude, "My partner needs the bitter medicine I'm dishing out in the form of bad attitudes and hurtful actions. Therefore, my raunchiness is justified." No way!

Instead your response should be, "Thank you, God, for making me exactly right for my mate. Help me be that, in the most creative, non-destructive way possible." That kind of attitude will allow you both to grow. By assuming responsibility for change in yourself, you free your partner

19

to change.

Now, I admit this is a startling concept and, frankly, I am not entirely proficient in the application of it. However, I can see profound changes occurring in my own marriage through a willingness, on my part, to see God in everything. For longer than I care to admit, I resisted Lucille. Instead of joining God in His effort to use her as a means of helping me grow, I joined Satan in accusing her of being less than she should be. As a result, I made her feel guilty, empty, useless, even worthless. I insisted that she change. Translated in her mind, this meant, "Be like me. Think as I think. Do as I do. Speak as I speak. Act as I act."

I have come to see I was wrong. Dead wrong. And I now praise God that I never succeeded in my persistent efforts to change her. If I had, it would have been a tragic loss. The world doesn't need two of me! What it needs is one of each of us living and growing as God intended. So I'm learning to praise Him for those few things in her nature which I find annoying, because they are exactly what I need, exactly when I need them.

May I be so bold as to suggest that the marriage mate God gave you is exactly right for you? Now, any marriage counselor worth his salt would readily attack the non-particularity of that statement. And rightly so. However, many Christians are being deprived of God's best by society's easy acceptance of separation and divorce. Without knowing the details of your situation, may I urge you to honestly and courageously examine the solution suggested here. To your blessing and benefit you may discover—as I have—it works!

The initial thing you need to do to turn what may be an unholy deadlock into holy wedlock is to learn to see God in everything and to open yourself to what He is trying to teach *you* through the person whom He has put closest to you. The person who is exactly right for you.

If you retreat from the irritations and annoyances of marriage through withdrawal into seclusion, physical separation, or even divorce, you will only force God to either raise up a new source of irritation, or worse yet, set aside His best for you. Because of His love for you, He doesn't want to do either. He only wants to make you like Jesus. He is using your marriage mate, your parents, your children to do it.

Let Him. No, do more than that. Help Him. Encourage Him. Cooperate with Him. Thank Him. Praise Him. In this way you will turn your irritations into blessings and you will deprive Satan of one of the best methods he has for tearing up the body of Christ and destroying its effectiveness on earth.

You may feel your situation is impossible. You started wrong and you think it's too late to start right. Don't believe it. It is never too late to do things God's way. There has never been a marriage that could not have ended in failure, nor one that could not have been made a success.

For you to succeed in your so-called impossible situation requires that you get your ears unplugged, your mind open, your will surrendered and your attitudes healed.

It also requires that you stop being concerned about your rights and commit yourself to what is right.

Like Adam and Eve, you may be the victim of confused priorities. But God is ready to move into your present situation and use your brokenness to bring wholeness. There is a way to rebuild that relationship and you should start trying.

If you are separated, I am not suggesting that you rush back into a precipitous reconciliation. To do so would be futile. You would only repeat the same old mistakes. I am suggesting, however, that whether you are living together or not, you start taking some first steps.

Anything ever constructed started with a first. A first foundation stone. A first building block. A first nail. A first rivet. And the first step in rebuilding a broken relationship is to set your own house in order by putting God above everything and learning to see God in everything so you become a stronger, better person yourself.

The principle of fullness before overflow. Out of a healthy, openhearted, loving relationship with God may come the overflow of a growing, maturing relationship with your mate. You may yet be able to join Paul in saying: "Thanks be unto God, who always causeth us to triumph in Christ" (II Corinthians 2:14 KJV).

I believe, with all my soul, that even the most shaky marriage can be made sturdy and stable if each of the partners will learn to pray something like this:

"Thank You, Lord, for making me exactly what my mate needs. Help me to be that, in the most creative, non-destructive way possible. And thank You, Lord, for making my mate exactly what I need. I praise You, Lord, that You are in everything, even the irritations and annoyances of life. Form the pearl of a more Christlike character in me so that, as I change, my partner will be free to change because the need for the growth-producing sand will no longer exist. Change this marriage, Lord, beginning with me. In Jesus' name, Amen."

2
The Principle of
What It's For

Somewhere I read about a chap who had the bad habit of leaving the keys in his car. One day while he was at home, he heard a car door slam, an engine start, and as he looked out his front window he saw someone steal his automobile. He rushed outside to try to stop the thief.

When he came back into the house, his wife asked, "Did you catch him?"

"No," he said glumly. Then brightening somewhat he added, "But I got his license number!"

Obviously the poor fellow didn't understand his problem. But in a roundabout way, he's illustrative of a lot of Christian people who sense something's wrong with their marriage, but they aren't quite sure what it is. And, like our befuddled hero, their efforts at solving the situation are usually far too superficial.

Therefore, it is imperative that you learn to look at your marriage from God's perspective so you can see what He had in mind when He designed this relationship and what needs He meant for it to fill.

When you look to scripture you may discover, perhaps to your dismay, that there are tremendous differences between your expectations of marriage and the purposes God had for it. And it's here, at the point of expectations, that many marital disappointments are spawned.[1]

It's impossible to grow from infancy to adulthood without having some of your most basic needs frustrated. Your need for total acceptance, for instance. Or your need for complete approval and affection. Nor does the longing to have these basic needs satisfied weaken as you grow. If anything, it becomes stronger.

There is a tendency on the emotional level—though you might want to deny it on the intellectual level—to enter marriage with the expectation that now, at long last, your deepest needs are going to be met. But that's a myth. It simply isn't so. It was never God's intention for marriage to meet your deepest needs. And the more excessive your expectations, the greater your potential for frustration—even rage—at not having your most basic needs fulfilled.

That is why it's desperately important for you to master and be mastered by The Principle of Fullness Before Overflow, lest you look to "John" or "Jane" to satisfy the longings which lurk deep inside of you, rather than looking to Jesus for the basic need fulfillment He alone can give.

My concern in this book is for Christian marriage. And Christian marriage is quite different from marriage per se. They share some things in common, of course, but in other ways there are no similarities whatsoever. Therefore, if you want your home to be Christian, you must not look to society for guidance, but to scripture. For there, and there alone, you will find those principles which, if followed, will enable you to experience God's best.

It's important to note, at this point, that it takes more than two Christians to make a Christian marriage. There are many Christian couples living together in a legal relationship which falls far short of being Christian. They're good people. Intelligent people. Sincere people. Christian people. But their marriage is not Christian. It takes more than two married Christians to make a Christian marriage.

If you're looking for a definition, we might say that a Christian marriage is the mating of two people who have sought fullness before overflow: who have put God above everything and see God in everything; who have come to understand the purpose principle—what marriage is for from God's perspective—and have mutually agreed, with God's help, to live in harmony with God's purposes for their home. If you can accept that definition, the obvious question is, "What are the needs God meant a Christian marriage to meet?" The Bible spells out seven.

Completion

The first of these is that you and your mate might share the experience of completion. Look again at a portion of that landmark text we examined earlier in some detail. "Then the Lord God said, 'It is not good for the man to be alone: I will make a helper suitable for him'. . . For this cause a man shall leave his father and mother and shall cleave to his wife; and they shall become one flesh" (Genesis 2:18,24). There's a great mystery here. The mystery of how a wholeness can become more whole.

When Adam was involved in a genuine loving relationship with God, he enjoyed a blessed state of self-realization. He was a whole person. The atmosphere in which he lived was completely satisfying, from his point of view. But God, who had made him and knew him from head to toe, saw needs in Adam which Adam didn't perceive himself.

So God, not Adam, said, "It is not good that this man should be alone; I'll make a partner for him, and these two shall become one flesh" (author's paraphrase). That is to say, *this* one and *this* one shall become *one*.

Now, any way you look at that you have an interesting equation. It is not one plus one equals two. Nor is it one alongside one becomes eleven. It is, one times one makes one!

If you will mentally review those three arrangements, you'll discover that in each instance the factors, that is, the ones—or in the case of Adam and Eve, the persons involved—remain the same. But the end result of each ar-

25

rangement is profoundly different.

In the first, the ones become two. In the second, the ones become eleven. In the third, the ones become one. This is a mysterious merging of two separate but equal entities which so complement each other as to complete each other. With God above everything and in everything, Adam and Eve began as units of wholeness which, through the alchemy of marriage, found a form of completion in each other neither had experienced in their single state.

So the first purpose of Christian marriage, as revealed in scripture, is completion. Not competition. For while, through marriage, God made you and your partner one, if you ever try to figure out which one, you're in trouble!

A chap was about to celebrate his 25th anniversary. "Do you remember your wedding day?" he was asked.

"I sure do!" he answered. "I carried my bride across the threshhold of our tiny home and said, 'Honey, this is our little world. Yours and mine!' "

"Well," his friend inquired, "did you live happily ever after?"

"Not exactly," the fellow replied somewhat grimly, "we've been fighting for the world's championship ever since."

The two persons involved here may have been Christian, but their marriage wasn't. A Christian marriage is not concerned with competition, but with mutual completion. It is a source and center of fellowship, companionship, but best of all, friendship.

Unfortunately, many couples become lovers without becoming friends. When the chemistry is over, they discover they are either strangers or competitors or both.

If that happens to be true with you, there is something you can do about it. Start by realizing the best way to have a friend is to be a friend. The following definition has been attributed to C. Raymond Beran:

> What is a friend? I'll tell you. It is a person with
> whom you dare to be yourself. Your soul can be

naked with him. He seems to ask you to put on
nothing, only to be what you really are...When
you are with him...you do not have to be on your
guard. You can say what you think, so long as it
is genuinely you.

A friend understands those contradictions in
your nature which cause others to misjudge you.
With him you breathe freely. You can avow your
little vanities and envies...and absurdities, and
in opening them up to him they are dissolved in
the white ocean of his loyalty. He understands...You can weep with him...laugh with
him, pray with him. Through and underneath it
all he sees, knows and loves you. A friend, I
repeat, is one with whom you dare to be yourself.

A high standard? You bet. But one worth striving for
because your marriage deserves it. To make this work will
require that you keep your first love alive. The ability to
give true friendship to another requires that you enjoy the
loving, caring, giving friendship of God. Your sense of being somebody to Him will clear your mind of questions
about your own identity and worth so you can relate to
your mate in a healthy way.

A Spirit-filled friend is one who assiduously avoids the
temptation to push those buttons which bring out the
worst in you, and who prays, as we have said previously, to
be "exactly what my mate needs...in the most creative,
non-destructive way possible."

A husband wrote his wife a love letter, in which he said,
"My attention has been called to an anecdote about Henry
Ford. He used to ask folks, 'Who is your best friend?' As
they considered a reply, Ford would write the answer: 'The
person who brings out the best in you.' " The husband continued his love letter, "I thought about the story and
asked myself whose name I would use. Yours was the only
one which qualified!"

Let it be said again: A Christian marriage is not concerned with competition, but with mutual completion. It is a source and center of fellowship, companionship, but best of all, friendship. Perfect marriage is a friendship in which neither partner cares one whit about winning, but where both are committed to resolving each difference through a creative compromise in which neither wins at the expense of the other person's losing.

Everyone has a form of power. Everyone. There is husband power. Wife power. Parent power. Child power. And you can employ your power in such a fashion as to win. But every time you win, you lose, because something goes out of your relationship with the person who has lost. Instead of being more complete, you are less complete. Put simply, you pay too great a price for winning.

I was talking the other day with someone who said, in a kind of singsong fashion, "My partner and I have arguments, but they never last for long. In fact, they are over just the instant I admit I'm wrong."

My friend was kidding—I think—but the point is that Christian marriage was not made for competition. Its initial purpose is completion. Therefore, you must surrender the neurotic need to win lest you lose what God is trying to teach you through the irritation and annoyances spawned sometimes by the incredible intimacy of marriage.

Perfect marriage is not one in which there are no problems. It is one in which you and your partner have rejected the concept of marriage as competition and, seeing God in everything, understand that marriage is meant for your mutual growth and temporal completion.

Consolation

This prepares you to fulfill the second purpose God had in mind for marriage: The experience of mutual consolation. "I will make him a helper suitable for him," God said (Genesis 2:18). What a beautiful way of expressing the simple truth that everybody needs somebody, sometime! And that somewhere in this vast, impersonal world, there must be some place where the struggle can cease, and instead of facing confrontation, an individual can find consolation, comfort, solace and rest.

In an excellent little book entitled, *Contact: The First Four Minutes,* the author, Leonard Zunin, points out that there are two four-minute periods in a day which are absolutely critical to the maintenance of a happy marriage. They are the first four minutes upon awakening in the morning, and the first four minutes upon coming together in the evening after having been apart for the day.

He says these two small segments of time are so significant you should practice the most stringent personal disciplines to assure they are positive and creative in nature. If need be, he urges, fake a positive attitude during these two sets of four minutes because the first set determines what will happen throughout the day, and the other determines what will happen throughout the balance of the evening.[2]

Well, if you're a Spirit-filled Christian, you won't have to fake anything. You won't have to feign or pretend interest in your mate. You only have to recognize the critical importance of these two brief interludes. Remember, your basic commitment is to meet your partner's needs. Ask for the Holy Spirit's help to see your mate through the eyes of Jesus, and then let the joy of what Jesus sees in that person flow through you to him or her.

To be a helper fit for your spouse also means allowing him or her to let off steam, if need be, without personalizing the process and making yourself part of the problem. In fact, if there is one prayer every Spirit-filled Christian ought to pray repeatedly throughout the day, but especially prior to and during these critically important four-minute segments it's the simple prayer,

"Lord, keep me from becoming part of the problem.

"Let me be an instrument of Your peace."

If you allow yourself to become part of the problem, you become an ally of Satan, who is trying to create turmoil and chaos in your home. But, even worse, you deny God the privilege of using you as the channel of His healing grace.

All God needs in a home is one Spirit-filled Christian who refuses to become part of the problems experienced there, and the Heavenly Father will use that one child of His to move that home toward becoming a center of consolation rather than confrontation.

On the other hand, if you allow Satan to make you part of the problem by using you to accuse your mate of being less than he or she should be, everybody loses. Everybody, that is, but Big Red. That's a tragedy. Therefore, you must accept personal responsibility for your own tongue-training program. This is not something you can accomplish in the flesh. It will only come about as you place yourself under the control of the Holy Spirit.

The book of Proverbs describes the consolation which results when you master the art of creative listening and appropriate speaking. "A word fitly spoken is like apples of gold in pictures of silver" (Proverbs 25:11 KJV). How wonderful to say the right thing at the right time!

Communication

This brings us around to the third basic need God designed Christian marriage to fulfill: communication. A man was asked if he and his wife were among the many alienated couples we hear so much about. He answered with a shrug, "I don't know, we never talk!"

"It is not good that the man should be alone," God said, and it's a simple fact that there is no way to counter aloneness without communication.

This is true in your relationship with God. The aloneness

30

you experience when, like Adam and Eve, you are "in hiding" (Genesis 3:8), can never be alleviated without communication. Communication from Him to you, first of all, as He communicates the incredible good news that He accepts you. And then from you to Him, as you communicate back your willingness to be accepted.

Communication is the only counter for aloneness. There is no other way to do it. So when God saw it wasn't good for Adam, a very put-together person, to be alone, He established the relationship of marriage as a means of meeting this need to counter aloneness through communication.

Whenever we talk about communication, we generally think in terms of words. But your mate is more than a pair of ears that hear. He or she is also eyes which see, and a heart which feels. Therefore, communication involves facial expressions, vocal inflections, tone of voice, body language, all of which are part of an intricate communications system God has designed so you can hear and be heard; so your mate can become a part of your life, and you can become a part of his or hers.

That's not going to happen without some confrontation. No two people with even average intelligence are going to agree about everything all the time. *But being heard is not necessarily being agreed with. Being heard is being understood and affirmed; given the right to your opinion. And I might add, giving your mate the right to his or her opinion. In fact, as Sidney Harris, the widely-read columnist, has said, "Maturity begins when we're content to feel we're right without feeling the necessity of proving someone else is wrong."*

Communication through confrontation can be helpful and healing if it's by love, with love, and for love. It must be by love; that is, from someone who loves us. It must be with love; that is, expressed in a loving way. And it must be for love in that it has as its ultimate purpose the reassurance that we are loved.

31

Confrontation without love cannot achieve any of these objectives. It not only won't help; it will actually harm. At best, it will be an expression of rudeness. At worst, it will issue in brutality. Therefore, you desperately need to remember God's goal for you is communication, not rivalry or contention.

Because Christian marriage is essentially spiritual in nature, true communication occurs in the area of the spirit, not just the mind, emotions and will. This happens as you learn to pray together about your problems and mutually—as well as individually—practice The Principle of Fullness Before Overflow, thereby freeing yourselves from the natural tendency to hide or be secretive. As you learn to open yourselves to each other and genuinely seek God's best, you will grow in your ability to deal in a candid, loving way with the gut issues affecting your marriage. In the process, your sense of aloneness will be alleviated because the barriers between you and your partner will be down and bridges of understanding will be up.

Coition

The fourth thing marriage is for is coition or sexual fulfillment. The very first chapter of the Bible declares, "God saw all that He had made, and behold, it was very good" (Genesis 1:31). Included in what He had made was the human body with all its complex emotions, hungers and drives. God called these good. It was His desire that Adam and Eve should be naked and unashamed, because coition was the logical culmination of all of the other effective forms of communication He had opened to them.

In a Christian marriage, coition is not doing something; it is saying something. It is declaring, "Now that we are one, you are not alone. You are a vital part of me. I am a vital part of you. Without you there is something gone from me. And though it boggles my mind, without me, there is something gone from you."

Coition is a vital and tangible way of making it clear to your mate that he or she matters. Out of several billion people on the face of the earth, this one man, or this one woman, has been joined to you in such a way as to make possible the free expression of delight and joy which God knew coition would provide when He blessed it, called it good, and later said, "Marriage is honourable in all, and the bed undefiled" (Hebrews 13:4 KJV).

I urge you to use I Corinthians 7:3-5 as another helpful guide to a healthy expression of this part of your married life. I include it here—in a contemporary translation—as preparation for a more thorough discussion of the subject later on.

> The husband should give his wife what is due to her as his wife, and the wife should be as fair to her husband. The wife has no longer full rights over her own person, but shares them with her husband. In the same way the husband shares his personal rights with his wife. Do not cheat each other of normal sexual intercourse, unless of course you both decide to abstain temporarily to make special opportunity for fasting and prayer. But afterward you should resume relations as before, or you will expose yourselves to the obvious temptation of the devil (I Corinthians 7:3-5, J. B. Phillips).

Creation

The fifth basic need God had in mind when he ordained marriage as the basic building block of society was creation—the bringing of new life into being. This is a subject we shall deal with in more detail under The Principle of Sexuality. But it's neat to know, isn't it, that when you and your mate give yourselves to each other in the in-

33

timacy of Christian marriage, you not only celebrate your oneness in spirit but, by the simple act of joining bodies, become participants with God in the continuum of life.

Correlation

Now, the sixth and seventh purposes God has for Christian marriage are so wonderful they are almost beyond belief. To get hold of them you must turn to Ephesians 5. There you discover that, having fulfilled its purpose as a means of mutual completion, consolation, communication, coition and creation, God intends that the world shall be able to look at your Christian marriage and see a direct correlation between it and the Body of Christ—His Church.

Beginning with Ephesians 5:21, Paul gives precise instructions as to the kinds of relationships which are to exist within a Christian home. Again, we will talk about these in greater detail in subsequent chapters. But, as he brings his instructions to a close, Paul includes a quotation from the second chapter of Genesis. "For this cause shall a man leave his father and mother, and shall be joined unto his wife, and they two shall be one flesh" (Ephesians 5:31 KJV). Then he adds: "This is a great mystery: but I speak concerning Christ and the church" (verse 32).

As a Christian, your home is to be a microcosm of the Body of Christ. A "little church," as it were. A koinonia cluster. A fellowship so special in both substance and spirit, folks can safely say to their unsaved neighbors and friends, "Would you like to know what a Christian church is supposed to be like? Take a look at that home. Examine that couple. Study the lifestyle of those two people. That's it! That's the church in miniature. That's a living example of what being a Christian is all about."

Christianization

The seventh purpose God has for a Christian marriage is the Christianization of the world, by multiplying your one, living, motion picture of the church a million times over. No, a half-billion times over, which is the approximate number of professing Christian homes in the world today.

Can you imagine what would happen if all five hundred million of these professing Christian homes were inhabited by Spirit-filled Christians, so that not just the people but the marriages themselves, were truly Christian! That kind of practical, down-to-earth, everyday living witness would put Satan out of business overnight. And he knows it! That's why he has launched such a vicious attack upon Christian homes today. That is why he's subjecting God's people to such horrendous oppression.

When all is said and done, a truly Christian home is by far the most powerful and persuasive evangelistic agency on earth. Without ever passing out a tract, preaching a sermon, or even saying a word, a Spirit-filled Christian home witnesses by the atmosphere which pervades it. It declares to all who come within reach that God will do for others what He has done for them, if they'll only give Him a chance.

For any number of reasons, our world has become weary of words. But when the world sees marriage working, when it sees the people involved changing for the better, when it sees them turning irritations into blessings and being drawn closer and closer to each other, then, believe me, the world stops, looks and listens!

There isn't anyone anywhere who doesn't have a healthy hunger hidden away inside for the very things a Christian marriage is designed to give. And when you put that fact on the front bleachers of your mind where it can grab your attention and hold it, when you think about the magnificent picture God has given you in scripture of what a

Christian home was meant to be—a source and center of completion, consolation, communication, coition, creation, correlation and Christianization of the world—can't you see how Satan must be ecstatic, absolutely convulsed with perverse glee, at the turmoil and chaos he is creating in the homes of many Christians today!

Can't you understand how grossly sinful it is for two Christian people to live together in a way that is not truly Christian!

Can't you see that the worst sin—the sin most common to Christians—is not anything society would consider illegal or immoral, it's the sin committed inside the home. The demeaning and destructive things said and done to each other which so grieve the Holy Spirit He cannot and will not fill us and use us as He could!

Can't you see, therefore, why you absolutely must learn to abhor evil and cleave to that which is good!

Can't you see why it's so terribly important that you determine, at least for yourself, that you will not let Satan win, but will offer yourself as a channel through which God's grace can flow into your home and through your home to the lives and homes of others!

A six-year-old was being taught how to pray. After spelling out a few basic guidelines, his Sunday School teacher suggested they pause for a few moments of prayer itself. "Perhaps we ought to pray about something very close to you," she suggested. "Your home, for instance. Get comfortable in your chair," she said. "Bow your head. Close your eyes. Settle down until things are quiet inside. Think about your home and how things are going there. Then tell God what your home needs."

After a few moments of silence, the curly-haired, six-year-old whispered ever so fervently, "Help!"

I believe most, if not all of us would want to join him in his prayer. And few, if any of us could express our heart's desire with greater eloquence or brevity. Knowing marriage as God meant it to be requires mutuality expressed in loving support and involvement. But, praise God, what you and your mate want for yourselves in your marriage is nothing compared to what God is waiting to give if both of you will put Him above everything, see Him in everything, and let Him begin molding your marriage into what it is meant to be.

Are you afraid to let go and let God rule your home? You needn't be. The ancient axiom is as true today as it was when it was first expressed: "God always gives His best to those who leave the choice to Him."

3

The Principle of Equality With Diversity

"Then God said, 'Let us make man [neuter gender, meaning mankind] in our image, according to our likeness; and let *them* rule over the fish of the sea and over the birds of the sky and over the cattle and over all the earth, and over every creeping thing that creeps on the earth.' And God created man [neuter gender] in His own image, in the image of God He created him; *male and female He created them.* And God blessed *them;* and God said to *them,* 'Be fruitful and multiply, and fill the earth, and subdue it; and rule over the fish of the sea and over the birds of the sky and over every living thing that moves on the earth' " (Genesis 1:26-28, italics added for emphasis).

It is clear from the reading of the above scripture that The Principle of Equality With Diversity is basic to a proper understanding of marriage from God's perspective. It is symbolized in the graphic by two wedding rings. Each complete in itself, depicting equality; yet each differing from the other in substance and appearance, suggesting diversity.

These two qualities must be kept in proper tension, for the Bible declares that male and female were both created in the image of God and given a common commission by God to perform as equal partners in: (1) the area of family life—they are to "be fruitful and multiply"; and (2) in carrying out God's plan for the earth—they are to "subdue it" and "have dominion over [it]."

As David Augsburger says so well, "Male and female were created in the image of God. Equally. Two parts of one unity, man. Man—he, and man—she, as the Hebrew of Genesis 1:26,27 expressed it."[1]

As God viewed Adam and Eve, He saw them as two parts of human personhood. Each was whole in Him. Each experienced a blessed state of self-realization. Yet each through the mysterious alchemy of marriage, was able to contribute something to the other. God's ideal for them was not duplication. They were two separate and distinct people who became a unity.

But their oneness was not meant to negate their two-ness. Each was to retain his or her individuality, and, by making the most of their diversity, discover their full potential as persons.

Satan Perverts God's Plan

What happened to God's beautiful idea? Sin happened. Genesis 3 explains that, as a consequence of the fall, the Principle of Equality With Diversity was subverted by evil. Equality was lost in a struggle for supremacy. Diversity was stained with perversity. The sweet communion Adam and Eve had known in the garden with God and each other was shattered.

Genesis 3:16 records one of the more famous of God's pronouncements to women. "...your desire shall be for your husband, and he shall rule over you." A much better translation is used in the Jerusalem Bible. "He will lord it over you."

What we have here is not a prescription in which God consigns women to a subordinate role forever. Rather it is a description of how Adam, streaked with sin, will take advantage of Eve and, as her husband, will attempt to dominate or lord it over his wife.

This leads us to an obvious conclusion. The concept of man as superior, and woman as inferior, is not representative of God's ideal. Instead, it is indicative of just how badly Satan has perverted that ideal.

Christ Comes to Right All Wrongs

But there's hope. Genesis 3:16 is not God's final word regarding the relationship between the sexes. Galatians 3:28 declares that in Christ all the old stereotypes are set aside. "There is neither Jew nor Greek, there is neither slave nor freeman, there is neither male nor female; for you are all one in Christ Jesus."

This electrifying declaration that in Christ all of the encumbrances of the fall are revoked and any distinction between the sexes is erased, is stated elsewhere in scripture. "In (the plan of) the Lord and from His point of view woman is not apart from and independent of man, nor is man aloof from and independent of woman; for as woman was made from man, even so man is also born of woman. And all (whether male or female) go forth from God as their author" (I Corinthians 11:11,12, *The Amplified Bible*).

First Peter 3:7 refers to husbands and wives as fellow-heirs of the grace of life, and Colossians 3:1-11 declares, "If then you have been raised up with Christ [i.e., genuinely and thoroughly been born again into this new lifestyle], keep seeking the things above . . . not on the things that are on earth. For you have died and your life is hidden with Christ in God . . . put them all aside: [there follows a whole list of the consequences of the fall], since you laid aside the old self with its evil practices, and have put on the new self who is being renewed to a true knowledge according to the image of the One who created him, a renewal [in this new order which is really a return to God's original ideal as spelled out in Genesis 1 and 2] in which there is no distinction between Greek and Jew, circumcised and uncircumcised, barbarian, Scythian, slave and freeman, but Christ is all, and in all."

It is a fact, you see, that when Jesus conquered sin through His death and resurrection, He accomplished far more than most of us have ever realized. He not only took away guilt and its consequences, He also began to set right *all* the relationships sin had made wrong.

After the fall, as Genesis 3:16 explains, Adam began to lord it over Eve, turning sour the relationship God had designed to be sweet. But since Christ's death for sin, and through the power of His resurrection, Jesus has created a whole new breed of men and women whom He has put back in the garden, so to speak, where, by setting God above everything and seeing God in everything, they are free to discover, achieve and enjoy God's ideal for marriage and the home.

Part of the good news—a part which is often overlooked incidentally—is that Jesus reactivated The Principle of Equality With Diversity, so that together a man and wife can breathe the fresh air of God's freedom and experience His best for them. Where Jesus is, there is the potential for unity through equality with diversity.

In other words, under the Lordship of Jesus, and with the fullness of the Holy Spirit, both male and female are free—truly free—to acknowledge and live by the biblical Principle of Equality With Diversity, thereby experiencing the blessed unity which follows.

What It Means to Be Head

Perhaps you are wondering about the "head texts" scattered throughout scripture, for example, those verses which speak of man as "head of his wife." We will look at these in greater detail in subsequent chapters. When we do you will see that scripture does not contradict itself. Taken in their context, and properly applied, these verses are rich in meaning.

For instance, Ephesians 5:23,25 says, "For the husband is the head of the wife, as Christ also is the head of the church...husbands, love your wives, just as Christ also loved the church and gave Himself up for her." As you can readily see, the theme here is not control; it is love. Paul is not setting up an organizational chart. He is describing to men what it means to be a man.

True masculinity doesn't have anything to do with "machismo" about which we hear so much today—that phony masculinity characterized by bulging biceps and brilliance in bed. It means living out, as Jesus did, a caring, sacrificing, purifying, unchanging, self-giving love which is not only willing and anxious, but determined to lay everything, including one's self, on the line for the sake of one's beloved. *That's what it means for a man to be head, because that is what it meant for Jesus to be head.*

It's not a matter of dictatorial control, but of submissive, self-giving, self-humbling service. Let's look at the Gospel of Luke as Jesus cuts through our contorted ideas of headship with surgical precision. "Among the heathen it is their kings who lord it over them, and their rulers are given the title of 'benefactors.' But it must not be so with you! *Your* greatest man must become like a junior and your leader must be a servant...[for] *I* am the one who is the servant among you" (Luke 22:25-27, J. B. Phillips).

For a man to be head, then, means something far different than we have traditionally assumed. It means following the example of Jesus "who, although He existed in the form of God, did not regard equality with God a thing to be grasped, but emptied Himself, taking the form of a bond-servant...humbled Himself by becoming obedient to the point of death, even death on a cross" (Philippians 2:6-8).

That is what it means for a man to be a man. *That* is what it means for a man to be head. For *that* is what being *true* man and *true* head meant for Jesus.

Equal But Not the Same

Look again at The Principle of Equality With Diversity. To say you and your mate are equal is not to say you are the same. Many who are trying to escape the sexual stereo-types which our fallen nature spawned and society con-doned—even encouraged over the years—seem to have a hangup at this point. But the two of you do not have to be alike to be equal. Indeed, you should rejoice in your diversi-ty and individuality. These characteristics were designed and desired by God when He made you and gave each of you to the other.

Inasmuch as we shall deal with the diversity of male and female in Chapter Six, let's focus our attention now on your equality. In that regard, as we look at marriage from God's perspective, all thoughts, suggestions, implications and intimations of superiority or inferiority must be set aside. In God's eyes, you and your spouse are equal—period. There are diversities, to be sure, and you must not be afraid to face up to and deal with them. But before you can do this creatively and objectively, you must come to terms with your equality as you learn to look at each other through the eyes of Jesus.

Equal Racially

There are many things we might say about your equality in Christ, but let me mention three. As born-again Chris-tians seeking God's best for your lives, you and your mate enjoy racial equality because God designed it and desired it that way. By racial equality, I am not thinking of color or ethnic background (though I heartily affirm equality in these areas). I am highlighting your essential humanity, your equality as fellow members of the human race.

In his book, *Design for Christian Marriage*, Dwight Small emphasizes the New Testament's consistent equalitarian and democratic view of marriage when he writes, "There cannot be true oneness except as there is equal dignity and status. The wife who came from man's side is to stand at his side to share every responsibility, and to enjoy every privilege."[2] This is God's ideal.

When God gave Eve to Adam, and Adam to Eve, He gave each of them a human being, not an object to perform the functions of a human being. Therefore, God's ideal for marriage is not that it be reduced to an arrangement in which your partner performs certain functions for you. Money earner. Cheap laborer. Erotic pacifier.

In Christian marriage, God binds you to a person, not just his or her function. A person who, with God above everything and in everything, is exactly right for you. A person through whom God can channel His best to you. A Christian marriage is the mating of two people who are racially equal in terms of their essential humanity, for the Bible says, "male and female created He *them,* and God blessed *them,*" as co-equals.

Now I know there are some who make a great deal of the fact that Adam was created before Eve, implying that this means man is superior and woman is inferior. My response to that is: Read your Bible. If precedence of creation implies importance of standing, then animals are superior to humans because they were created first. But the Bible is clear in teaching that mankind, male and female, is the crown of God's creation.

There are others who make much of the fact that throughout scripture God is spoken of as "He." This means, they argue, God is masculine, which automatically makes man superior to woman. Those who teach this fail to reckon with the limitations of human speech and the fact that there aren't *any* words which adequately describe God as He is. They also overlook the many times when God uses both masculine and feminine illustrations in scripture in reference to Himself (Isaiah 42:14; 43:3; 49:15; 66:13; Psalms 132:2, for example).

When the Lord Jesus, who was God incarnate in human flesh, stood above the city of Jerusalem and wept for its lostness, He used a maternal image to describe His feelings in that moment. "How often I wanted to gather your children together, the way a hen gathers her chicks under her wings..." (Matthew 23:37).

And while you undoubtedly recognize the waiting father in the parable of the prodigal son and the shepherd who goes searching for the one lost sheep as being representative of God, have you paused to think of the woman who diligently swept out her entire house in search of a single stray coin as being representative of God? And yet, if you're going to be true to scripture, you have to face the fact that all three of these parables are found in the very same chapter, side by side, and came from the lips of none other than the Son of God Himself (Luke 15:1-32).

The simple truth is, God is neither masculine nor feminine. As Jesus told the woman at the well, "God is spirit" (John 4:24). In His spirit are encompassed qualities found in both sexes. Therefore, women as well as men have the right to think of themselves as having been made in God's image to share equality before Him.

Equal Relationally

Along with a racial equality, as two born-again Christians seeking God's best for your lives, you and your mate share relational equality in the Lord, as we read earlier in I Corinthians 11, Colossians 3, Galatians 3, and I Peter 2.

I'm convinced, after much prayer and meditation upon scripture, that all the laws and legalities laid down in the Bible are God's accommodation to our fallen nature, and fall far short of fulfilling His ideal as spelled out in Genesis

45

*1 and 2—equality in all relationships with God above
everything and in everything.*

In a relationship between two unsaved people, or between a Christian and non-Christian, these laws and
legalities can be very helpful. But my concern in this book
is for Christian marriage. There is no biblical support for
those who insist the man must lead in all practical and
spiritual matters in the marriage of Spirit-filled Christians
regardless of his ability, simply because he was born male.

When we begin to talk this way, some folk get all shook
up because they are afraid we might disobey scripture, or
create social chaos. But as we've already seen in part, and
as we shall see more fully in subsequent chapters, passages
of scripture which seem to suggest a chain of command
based on rank—masters-slaves, rulers-subjects, men-
women—are simply an accommodation by God to the
fallen nature of mankind.

Efforts to crystallize these into ironclad arrangements
for all Christians and for all time, fail to grasp the wonderful truth of what it means to be fellow citizens in the kingdom of God. Or what it means to walk in the newness of
life. Or what it means to be part of a new order in which all
the cultural, social and sexual distinctions simply have no
significance.

As Christians, whether we be master or slave, ruler or
subject, man or woman, we are one. We enjoy relational
equality in the Lord. We stand together on level ground
before the cross as sinners saved by grace.

Equal Responsibility

As two born-again Christians seeking God's best for
your lives, your marriage is not only an experience of racial
equality in the sense of your both being fully human, and
relational equality in that you both stand on level ground
in the Lord, but it is also a responsible equality, in that you

both are accountable to the Lord for your own spiritual and emotional hygiene.

Christian marriage is a relationship between two of God's children in which the independence is equal, the interdependence is mutual, and the responsibility is reciprocal.

Christian marriage is a journey into full maturity. Maturity is marked by a willingness to assume responsibility. This includes, among other things, responsibility for your own spiritual and mental hygiene. Only then can God make you whole. Only then can He keep you from becoming a spiritual or psychic vampire who sucks the energy you need for survival from your mate.

Earlier I said the equation which best describes Christian marriage is, one times one equals one. When I tried that out on one of my friends who has a mathematical bent, she pointed out that one-half times one-half does not remain one-half. It reduces to one-quarter. She went on to explain the insight the Lord had given to her: *If two incomplete, or non-whole people join together in marriage, they actually become less than they were when they were single.* One-half times one-half becomes one-quarter.

She shared the fact that while God had made it clear she could not change her unsaved mate from one-half to one, that is, from a person who is less than whole to a person made whole by the Lord Jesus, she had an individual responsibility for her own halfness as an ofttimes carnal Christian. It became clear to her that if she would allow God to *be* God in her life, so He could change her from one-half to one by making her whole through the fullness of the Spirit, her marriage would improve one hundred percent.

The equation she wrote out was as follows: one-half times one-half equals one-quarter. One-half times one equals one-half. That represents a hundred percent improvement! So now, instead of worrying about her husband whom she can't change anyway, she's focusing on her own personal responsibility before the Lord. She is opening herself to the wholeness which He alone can bring as He molds her and builds her into all she is meant to be. If her husband allows God to go to work in his life, too—what a marriage that would be! But at least she has begun where you, too, must begin—by accepting responsibility for your own personal relationship with God.

You cannot allow your spouse to do your religioning for you. The instant you do, God is not above everything. Your spouse is. You are asking of him or her what a human being cannot provide.

What is true spiritually is also true emotionally. A great deal is made of the fact that men live and work under tremendous pressure on their jobs—and we do, most of us. But women are oppressed, too, whether their vocation is outside or inside the home, or both.

A lady was doing some dusting when the telephone rang. In getting to the telephone, she tripped on a scatter rug, and, reaching out for something to hold on to, grabbed the telephone table which came over with a crash, dumping the phone on the floor, jarring the receiver off the hook. As the table fell, it hit the family dog which had been curled up asleep nearby. The dog yipped and howled and leaped around, upsetting the lady's four-year-old son who had come running in to see what was going on. In a state of shock the boy sat down on the floor and began screaming.

By this time, the lady had crawled to the receiver, picked it up and put it to her ear, just in time to hear her husband say, "Nobody has said 'Hello' yet, but I'm positive I've got the right number!"

Both male and female can be oppressed by life. Both are also streaked with lingering perversity as a result of our fallen nature.

I was chatting with a woman awhile back, and she said, "My husband and I have a perfect understanding. I don't try to run his life, and I also don't try to run my own."

Let it be said, there are some people who like it that way. They don't really want a Christian marriage—a marriage based on equality of responsibility. The other way is easier. They can go on manipulating and being manipulated.

The husband doesn't have to learn to love as Christ loved, and the wife doesn't have to give up her scapegoat. But the loss sustained in such a distorted relationship is tremendous. It not only keeps the individuals involved from becoming all they were meant to be, it deprives the world of an accurate picture of what the church is meant to be: a body of believers who reflect The Principle of Equality With Diversity in the Lord.

In summary, let's review the points we've covered thus far.

• The laws and legalisms laid down in scripture are a spin-off of our perversity, and were given by God to keep fallen mankind from totally devouring and destroying himself. They do not represent His ideal.

• The more mature you become in Christ, the less need you have for these temporal accommodations to your fallen nature.

• As you accept more and more responsibility for your own spiritual and emotional hygiene, you will begin to experience the beauty and blessedness of a marriage built upon The Principle of Equality With Diversity.

Before we proceed, however, may I confront you again with the fact of your responsibility for yourself before God. If you have never received Christ as your Savior; or, if you are born again, but have never set Him above everything and named Him Lord; or, if you are saved, but are not filled with the Holy Spirit (you are carnal one-half instead of Spirit-filled one); there is no better time than now to settle these vital issues. Until you allow the grace of God to act in your own life to make *you* whole, there can never be any hope of wholeness in your home.

4

The Principle of Responsible Headship

As two Christians desiring God's best for your marriage, one of the biggest challenges confronting you and your mate is learning to deal with real problems rather than wasting your time and energy in a futile attempt to solve what I call "non-problems." By non-problems I mean all those very painful, often quite perplexing situations and symptoms which grow out of misunderstanding due to insufficient information or inadequate communication.

Real problems can eventually be solved with enough wisdom, time and effort. Non-problems tend to become more distressing the harder you try to solve them.

A man rushed into a drugstore and asked for something to stop hiccups. The pharmacist casually poured a glass of water, turned unexpectedly and threw it into the man's face.

"What did you do that for?" the man exploded angrily.

"You don't have hiccups anymore, do you?"

"No!" shouted the customer, "but my wife out in the car still does!"

The Fallacy of Either/Or

In a homely fashion this little story brings us to the importance of dealing with the real problems besetting many Christian marriages. One of the more knotty is learning and understanding how the twin truths of authority and mutuality fit together. To show you just how real this problem is, a panoply of books has emerged with most of them opting for one or the other of these two prominent biblical truths relating to Christian marriage. Either the writer has defended the concept of masculine authority, or has presented the less familiar teaching of mutual submission. In both instances the authors seem compelled to deny, contort or ignore the so-called opposing truth. Amazing deductions are reached as, with genuine ingenuity, writers bob and weave to avoid the thrust of a teaching which appears to be at odds with the point they are attempting to make.

But when you approach scripture with an open heart and mind—free from preconceptions and presuppositions—you make a liberating discovery: *You are not limited to a choice between either authority or mutuality in your Christian marriage! In fact, it is my deep conviction both are essential to the kind of stability God desires for you, your marriage and your home. One of Satan's most clever deceptions is the suggestion you must choose between a purely authoritarian or purely equalitarian relationship. In my judgment both fall short of God's ideal for you. Both miss the beauty and strength achieved by a subtle but real blending of two powerful biblical truths.* Which is to say it's imperative—as you move toward perfect marriage—that you and your mate avoid the fallacy of *either/or.* You must not settle for *either* authority *or* mutuality. Instead, you must come to grips with God's *both/and* answer in which *both* authority *and* mutuality operate together in harmony to reinforce harmony.

God's Both/And Answer

To experience God's ideal for your Christian marriage, you must fully understand and actively implement the principle of mutual submission without disregarding the

Principle of Responsible Headship. Both are taught in scripture as illustrated in the following:

"Submit to one another out of reverence for Christ. Wives, submit to your husbands as to the Lord. For the husband is the head of the wife as Christ is the head of the church, his body, of which he is the Savior. Now as the church submits to Christ, so also wives should submit to their husbands in everything. Husbands, love your wives, just as Christ loved the church and gave himself up for her to make her holy, cleansing her by the washing with water through the word, and to present her to himself as a radiant church, without stain or wrinkle or any other blemish, but holy and blameless. In this same way, husbands ought to love their wives as their own bodies. He who loves his wife loves himself. After all, no one ever hated his own body, but he feeds and cares for it, just as Christ does the church—for we are members of his body. 'For this reason a man will leave his father and mother and will be united to his wife, and the two will become one flesh.' This is a profound mystery—but I am talking about Christ and the church. However, each one of you also must love his wife as he loves himself, and the wife must respect her husband" (Ephesians 5:21-33, NIV).

The twin truths taught in this passage call for mutuality ("submit to one another," verse 21) reinforced with responsible headship ("the husband is the head of the wife as Christ is the head of the church," verse 23) lived out in love ("husbands, love your wives, just as Christ loved the church," verse 25).

If you settle for either mutuality or authority—even when these are undergirded by love!—your marriage will miss the full potential inherent in a relationship based on God's *both/and* answer. *Both* authority *and* mutuality are taught in scripture. *Both* play a part in human relationships—especially those of perfect marriage—*and* both are to be exercised in love.

If your marriage is to be truly Christian and thus all you desire it to be, the prevailing atmosphere in which you live out that relationship will be one of mutuality. But mutuality must be reinforced with responsible headship expressed in the duality of obvious agape (selfless, Godlike, Calvary) love, and latent authority.

Now please stick with me. I've spent a ton of time listening to the voice of the Holy Spirit, asking Him to teach me how authority and mutuality fit together in Christian marriage. So you and I must "reason together" if I am to communicate effectively what I have learned.

If you're strong for authority and sold on submission, or if you're struggling with authority and soured on submission, you may really be stretched by what I'm about to say. All I ask is that you hear me out. By that I mean read with care and evaluate with prayer this chapter and the next on the Principle of Prevailing Atmosphere. If, after we've worked our way through the relevant biblical material, you still see it differently—fine. Let's agree to disagree. For now, please grant me the high honor of being heard.

Latent Authority: The Stabilizer of All Relationships

Deciding where to start is difficult because there is the possibility that reading half of what I've got to say may so turn you off you'll not play "the flip side of the record." But I must start somewhere, so let's begin with the nature of God Himself and the structure *He* established for the benefit of a fallen world.

The concept of authority is difficult to avoid in scripture. Authority is an integral part of who God is and what God

53

is doing through creation. By His nature God *is* authority. A quick reading of Genesis One followed by even casual reflection upon the oft-repeated statements: "God said . . . and it was so" (Genesis 1:6,7,9,11,14,15,24,26-30) reveal that an essential ingredient in God's nature is authority. He merely spoke and what He called for *occurred.* If that isn't the epitomy of unabridged authority I don't know what is.

Scripture not only teaches God *is* authority but that He reserves the right to delegate authority (Romans 13:1) and desires to lovingly exercise His authority for the benefit of His own (Isaiah 1:18-20; 55:6-9). And, of course, in a general overarching sense, God does graciously manage all things for the sake of believers through the profoundly simple process of using all things for good (Genesis 50:20; Romans 8:28-30). *However—and this is key—in a specific sense, God's authority is latent. That is, God's authority is always active, but not always apparent. A contemporary way of saying this is that God employs "laid-back authority."*

This does not mean God has abandoned His commitment to His creation (Psalms 23; 46; 91). What was meant to be in the beginning will be in the end (Genesis 3:15; Romans 8:28-30; Revelation 21:5-7). It simply means God has chosen to exercise His authority in a most fascinating and instructive way.

God has not revealed Himself as the Ultimate Adolescent needing to be "in control" at all times in an officious or meddlesome manner as a means of reassuring Himself He's okay. Instead, the God of scripture is shown to be Absolute Maturity able to risk *not* being "in control" in an obvious way, so *we* can learn He's okay. God allows us freedom of choice so we can discover He is righteous in the sense of being right with Himself. Whole, as well as being holy. Seeing God as Maturity with a capital "M" frees us to believe He can be trusted to love us no matter what. We find out He really does have a better idea as to how life works out best. We learn He cares about us. Cherishes us. Desires nothing but the best for us. As a consequence we freely, happily and deliberately respond to His laid-back authority. We *decide*—on our own—to let God *be* God. In the process we experience His best!

With this review of God's nature and behavior as the basis of our understanding, the concept of latent authority in perfect marriage comes into sharper focus. God is authority and all authority comes from Him. However, God exercises His authority in a way which is not apparent to the unpracticed eye. Had it been His plan to employ arbitrary authority, He could have achieved that objective much more efficiently and demonstrably by creating automatons which had no choice but to do His bidding. When He pushed "the love button, " His creatures would parrot, "I love you, God." When He pulled "the obedience string," His marionettes would, of necessity, involuntarily do as they were told. But there is no love in mannequins. No true obedience in robots. *Therefore, rather than go for efficiency in the form of puppets, God opted for effectiveness in the form of people to whom He gave the power of choice.*

In place of an instinctual interlock between creator and creation, such as operates in the animal kingdom, God equipped people with free will. He "backed off," so to speak, choosing to activate His authority in specific ways in the lives of specific people *by invitation only*!

"In many ways He will be good and kind,
But God will not force the human mind."

There are exceptions, of course, when an independent spirit or rebellious attitude are so virulent they threaten His master plan. Then God intervenes. Swiftly. Arbitrarily. Decisively. Illustrations are found in the flood (Genesis 7), the Tower of Babel (Genesis 11), the defeat at Ai (Joshua 7), the shattering demise of Ananias and Sapphira (Acts 5). For the most part, however, God's relationship with *people* is based upon what I call latent authority. It is active, but not obvious.

All other creatures great and small behave in certain ways because God tells them to. They are programmed instinctually. Not so with man. At least, not in the same sense or degree. It's true, as Augustine said, there's a God-shaped blank in the human heart which calls you to a higher destiny. That's why you are restless until you rest in Him. Even so, by an exercise of free will, you can override this spiritual "instinct." You may, if you wish, settle for a good deal less than God's best. *And God lets you do it!* That's the point I wish to make.

Releasing God's Best

If I understand God's purpose in creating mankind, it is that He desires fellowship with people who desire fellowship with Him. He longs for people who have learned life's most important lesson: things work out only one way—God's way! People who, therefore, deeply desire to know and do God's will. People who gladly submit to God's authority (His headship, if you will), because they know it represents His best. For them. For others. For everyone. In everything. In fact, as I see it, what God is aiming toward is the raising up of a whole new breed of people (Ephesians 2:1-22) who have learned in the School of Hard Knocks that life works out only when it is lived in *voluntary submission to God's loving authority.* And thus this new breed of people joyfully, voluntarily and deliberately decide to live life God's way. Forever!

The incredible part of God's plan is that when He has fully peopled heaven with individuals who are voluntarily committed to His living authority, following the example of Jesus in time, and are prepared to live in obedience to Him forever, it is God's will to share His glory with them—*forever* (John 4:34; 5:30; 6:38; 8:29; 15:10; Matthew 25:31-34; Mark 16:19; Luke 12:32; Romans 8:14-17; Galatians 4:7; Ephesians 1:18-23; 2:4-7; Philippians 3:20,21). I don't pretend to understand this. But the Bible teaches it. So I believe it and happily proclaim it.

Authority and the Church

This moves us to yet another stage in the reasoning process and requires that we think about authority and the church. In the Ephesians passage quoted earlier, Paul speaks of the relationship between a Christian husband and Christian wife as "a profound mystery." He has just said, "The husband is head of the wife, as Christ is head of the church" (Ephesians 5:23, NIV) and goes on to say, "I am talking about Christ and the church" (verse 32). I am in agreement, as I shall explain later, with the view that one meaning of "head," as used metaphorically in scripture, is that of "source." Jesus is the source of the church. It springs from Him and receives its life from Him. However, this does not relieve me as a Christian believer from the necessity of naming Jesus Christ as Lord. His Lordship is rooted in His authority (John 17:1,2; 3:35; Hebrews 1:1-14; I Peter 3:20,22; Philippians 2:9-11; Revelation 5:1-14). Like His Father, Jesus desires to lovingly exercise His authority on our behalf. But also, like that of His Father, Christ's authority is laid-back. It is active, but not always apparent.

Jesus Is Lord, not "Boss"

Make no mistake about it: Jesus is Lord of the church (Ephesians 4:1-13). But He is a most unusual Lord. His relationship with His body is "bossless" in that He never arbitrarily "calls the shots." Not now, at least! When He comes in the fullness of His glory, it will be different (Matthew 24:30). He who first came in the guise of suffering-servant will come again as reigning Lord. By then, however, Spirit-filled believers will have learned what life on this planet is designed to teach and will be in full agreement with His arbitrary display of unabashed authority.

Indeed, rather than being cause for alarm, the prospect of Christ's coming "with power and great glory" is, or most certainly should be, our blessed hope. For the present, however, His Lordship is characterized by laid-back authority to allow us time to learn, as He did, what obedience implies (Hebrews 5:8).

Having said that, I must emphasize that while the Father, Son and Holy Spirit have chosen to employ latent authority, their authority is active. Authority is an integral and inescapable part of God's method of operation designed to foster order in a fallen world and help His children learn obedience.

Jesus Christ is Lord. Let there be no doubt of that. He has authority over the church. But He does not assume the posture of "boss." Why? Because it won't work. Human nature being what it is—fallen—causes us to bow our back when authority is expressed arbitrarily. We must learn obedience. More often than not we must learn it the hard way. But learn it we must. And that's what our days upon this planet are all about: learning to happily and voluntarily submit to God's authority. This is probably best done by learning to happily and voluntarily submit to the authority He has delegated.

Structure, Authority and Order

Call it what you like. Managing. Ruling. Leading. Protecting. Modeling. Authority is clearly taught in scripture. It cannot be ignored. It is part of the structure of things established by God Himself and is probably best understood in the light of a loving Father's concern for order. God is not the author of confusion (I Corinthians 14:33).

He has created and sustains an orderly universe (Psalm 136:3-9). One you can count on. Plan on. Build on.

It is incredible to discover the inordinate care with which the Heavenly Father has ordered His handiwork. God is not scatterbrained. Nor did God create a helter-skelter universe. The nature of things as God created and sustains them is remarkably cyclical and predictable. The order and symmetry which are part and parcel of God's person are not only evident in what He made but are clues to how He desires what He made to function.

Delegated Authority and the Maintenance of Order

This concern for order helps us get a handle on the concept of delegated authority. For instance, the Father gave the Son responsibility for reconciling the world unto Himself (II Corinthians 5:19). He also delegated to His Son the necessary authority to do that for which He had been made responsible.

Jesus explained He would lay down His life. He made it clear no one could take it from Him. He would lay it down, He said, on His own initiative. "I have authority to lay it [My life] down, and I have authority to take it up again. This commandment I received from My Father" (John 10:18). Jesus was *under* authority and at the same time *had* authority.

Currently God has delegated to the Holy Spirit the responsibility and equivalent authority to "convict the world concerning sin, and righteousness and judgment" (John 16:8). The Holy Spirit has also been given the task of teaching about Jesus, reminding of Jesus, guiding into Jesus, speaking for Jesus and glorifying Jesus (John 14:26; 16:13,14). He does all this as One who is under authority and yet has authority. "He [the Holy Spirit] will not speak on His own initiative [that is to say, He is under authority],

59

but whatever He hears, He will speak; and He will disclose to you what is to come" (John 16:13b). The Holy Spirit is *under* authority, while at the same time He *has* authority delegated to Him for ministry by the Father.

The same principle of delegated authority—people who are *under* authority and yet *have* authority—relates to civil leaders (I Timothy 2:2), parents (Ephesians 6:1,2), employers (Ephesians 6:5-9), spiritual leaders (II Corinthians 10:8; 13:10; Hebrews 13:17) *and, by inference, husbands.*

God's concern for order extends to seeing that a household is managed well. One criterion for being a spiritual leader is knowing how to maintain order in one's home (I Timothy 3:4). With this thought in mind, we can reach certain helpful conclusions. Not the least of these is that a Christian husband, like his model, the spiritual leader, is *not* required to do everything himself. It simply means God has given him the responsibility *and equivalent authority* to see that everything is managed. Our English word "husband" comes from an ancient phrase: "house-band." It has to do with keeping things together. As "house-band" a Christian husband is to "manage his household well." If he is wise he will delegate by mutual agreement various areas of responsibility and authority to his mate. But ultimate accountability lies with him. He *has* authority, but like his Savior Jesus he is *under* authority.

Ephesians 5:25 places a Christian husband under divine mandate to love his wife just as Christ loved the church. If that means anything at all, it means he is directed to accept responsibility for her in ways similar to the loving responsibility with which Jesus surrounds and undergirds His church. It means accepting responsibility to live a life of uncommon sacrifice which puts flesh on the words "I love you." It means accepting responsibility to develop and maintain a nonjudgmental atmosphere which frees his wife to become all she's meant to be. Above all, it means mastering and employing the duality of obvious agape love and latent authority involved in the principle of responsible headship.

I was discussing this the other day with a friend who is deeply committed to the concept of mutual submission in Christian marriage. He and his wife have established a beautiful relationship based upon operational equality in all things. He was really struggling with why there is a need for authority in his marriage, and if there *is* a need how it would work out. I told him I had observed authority operating in his home and, as far as I could tell, it was beautifully laid-back as authority should be.

"Let's talk about that for a moment," he said, "because I'm not sure I understand what you mean by latent, or laid-back, authority. For instance," he went on, "usually when this issue comes up, and I ask for a concrete illustration, reference is made to a couple driving down a highway. They come to a fork in the road, and a decision has to be made as to which way they will go. Invariably I'm told the man should make the decision. And I suppose if he's driving that's true. But if my wife were driving, I'd want *her* to make the decision."

"But suppose each of you had good reasons for going different routes?" I asked. "Suppose you had never been in this area; there are two routes you can take to reach your destination, and each of you has a strong preference for one route rather than the other?"

"Then," he replied, "I'd want us to pull off to the side of the road, talk about our differences and arrive at a decision with which both of us could be happy."

I thought about that a bit and then responded, "That's a perfect illustration of the principle of responsible headship in action! Recognizing a difference of opinion and the validity of both points of view, *you accept the responsibility to be responsible for maintaining the spirit of unity in the bond of peace and in a loving, caring way initiate* a conversation aimed at a negotiated settlement in which neither of you wins at the expense of the other person's losing. To me that is laid-back authority at its best.

"Now," I continued, "there's no reason why your wife couldn't initiate this problem-solving process. In your Spirit-filled marriage she not only could but maybe even would. The point I want to make is that, as husband, you would be willing and ready to initiate a conversation aimed at a decision with which both of you could be happy. And that's laid-back authority at its best!

"Maybe, as an act of sacrificial, self-giving love in the style of Jesus you say, 'Honey, I really want to go the other way. There are things along that route I'd like to see. But I want this to be a pleasant experience for you, too, so let's go your way. Maybe there'll be an opportunity when we can come back again and then we'll go my way...if not, it won't be the end of the world.'

"Perhaps your wife would take the initiative and make such an offer, and that would be neat, too. But if I understand what it means for a husband to be head of his wife, that is, in a manner similar to the way Christ is head of the church, it means *a Christian husband is the loving initiator*. He is the first to step forward with an offer of conciliation and submission out of reverence for Christ in her."

"I like that," my friend said. "The idea of initiating a loving encounter so we are both happy with the decision reached resonates with my understanding of latent authority as Jesus exercises it on behalf of the church. That's not only something I could do but something I very happily *would* do on behalf of my mate."

Well—we were really getting excited about God's *both/ and* answer for Christian marriage, and I said, "Let me try an illustration on for size. Marriage is often referred to as embarking on a voyage across the Sea of Matrimony. Such a voyage implies a vessel. Let's follow that imagery for a moment and think of the marriage relationship itself as a vessel.

"In building a ship, the first thing laid is the keel. Its function is to steady the ship and to keep it from capsizing. This is the opposite of seeing God *above* everything. However, seeing God *under* everything, as the starting point of everything—as that factor in the equation of marriage which makes everything stable and steady—is no less graphic."

My friend nodded his agreement.

"The first thing attached to the keel," I continued, "is a section of what will become the outer skin or plating of the vessel. Ultimately, when the ship is finished, that plating will rise high above the waterline and will become the beautifully finished surface which is seen and admired as it cuts through the water. So, right from the beginning, along with the keel as the primary stabilizer, there is concern for the appearance of the finished product. That's an interesting part of the process, as I'll point out in a moment.

"But before the outer skin or plating can rise very far, the interior ribs, or framing, which run transverse from the keel to the deck, must be added. The precise sequence in which this is done depends on the type of vessel being built. But the internal framework, or ribs—that which later becomes the unseen, mostly sub-surface, internal structure—must be there if the vessel is to stay together.

"Obviously, unless the outer plating is also added, the internal framing won't float on its own. Launch a ship which consists of nothing but the keel and ribs, and that baby will head straight for the bottom! It takes *both* internal framing *and* external plating for the ship to be complete. Most of the time, when the sailing is smooth, the unseen internal structure quietly does its job. It doesn't even squeak or groan. All you see is this gleaming white surface cutting cleanly and smoothly through the water.

"But let a storm develop—let that ship face 40-foot waves and a 70-mile-per-hour gale—and those aboard can be grateful that an unseen internal framework supports and strengthens that beautiful but ever so thin outer plating buffeted by the storm."

Enthused by the way my comparison was developing, I said to my friend, "Now then, as I see it, that's how authority and mutuality fit together in Christian marriage. With a loving heavenly Father as the keel providing overall steadiness to the Ship of Matrimony, mutuality is the external surface which is seen and observed of men. As in building a ship, *a commitment to mutuality must be made by the couple at the very beginning of their relationship*, because it is the prevailing atmosphere in which that relationship will be lived out on a day-to-day basis. It is also that which enables the world to see the connection between a Christian home and the Christian church. (See "Correlation" in Chapter Two.) Latent authority is the unseen support system which gives strength and stability to the outer surface. Most of the time it's just there—functioning faithfully like the ribs of a ship—but in those times that marriage is subjected to unusual stress, authority plays an important part in helping things hang together. Authority doesn't become more active, it just becomes more apparent. Its importance is more obvious. Its function is more fully appreciated.

"Now this is just an illustration," I added, "and, like all illustrations, it has certain limitations. But what do you think? Does this help you see how authority and mutuality fit together in God's both/and answer for Christian marriage?"

"Yes," said my friend. "Preach it! Perhaps it will help others also understand how authority and mutuality fit together and why a Christian husband must be ready to accept responsibility to be responsible and maintain the spirit of unity in the bond of peace."

More on the Meaning of Head

Having mentioned latent authority, let me address the subject of obvious agape love as it relates to a husband being head of his wife as Christ is head of the church. To begin with, for a husband to be head of his wife doesn't have anything to do with control, but has everything to do with love. It means living out, as Jesus did, a caring, sacrificing, purifying, unchanging, self-humbling, submissive love, which is not only willing but actually determined to lay everything, including one's self, on the line for the sake of his beloved. That's what it meant for Jesus to be head of the church; that's what it means for a husband to be head of his wife. It's not a matter of dictatorship, but of submissive self-giving, self-humbling service.

Look at Ephesians 5 again, this time starting at the beginning of verse 25 (NIV). "Husbands, love your wives, just as Christ loved the church and *gave himself up* for her . . ."; skipping down to verse 28, even so "husbands ought to love their wives *as their own bodies.* He who *loves* his wife loves himself" (italics added for emphasis).

What Paul says here is revolutionary. It may be difficult for some of us to comprehend exactly *how* revolutionary. We are the inheritors of nearly 2,000 years of Christian impact upon social structures, systems and thinking. We often take many things for granted. For instance, the idea that love is the reason a man marries a woman.

Even a cursory reading of ancient history shows that hasn't always been so. Excursions into sections of the world where there has been little, if any, penetration by the gospel reveal it *still* isn't so.

Love—as we Westerners employ the word—was rarely the reason a man married in the first century A.D. It was primarily to carry on his name. So, for Paul to say "husbands, *love* your wives" was a surprising, if not downright stunning statement.

But for him to add: love your wife *as your own body,* that is, love her as *yourself,* was mind blowing! This meant elevating her to a position of equality. It meant accepting her as one worthy of as much attention and concern as he gave to himself. It meant thinking of her as a person of equal significance, worth and value. To a first-century male this was an absolutely revolutionary concept. It is almost as surprising to some of our contemporaries who still do not fully comprehend what Paul meant when he spoke of a Christian husband being head of his wife.

It may come as a surprise to you, but as used metaphorically in the New Testament "head" has little to do with ruler or the act of ruling. Colossians 2:9,10 speaks of Jesus and declares: "For in Him all the fullness of Deity dwells in bodily form, and in Him you [all Christians] have been made complete, and He is the head over all rule and authority." The use of the word "over" in our English texts suggests rulership. However, a careful review of the Greek text reveals that "head" means source. That is, Jesus is the source of all rule and authority. Romans 13:1 says all authority comes from God. As God incarnate, Jesus represents and in fact is the source of all rule and authority. Colossians 2:10 says that, as a Christian, you are one with that source. You derive your fullness from Jesus when you are in Jesus from Whom all fullness flows.

The idea of "head" as being the same as "source" turns up in Ephesians 5:23 where we read, "Christ also is the head of the church, He Himself being the Savior of the body [that is, the body's source of life!]."

As used metaphorically in the New Testament, "head" does not point to the top spot on the organizational chart of a corporation. It refers to a loving and living unity. A one-flesh relationship which springs from the fact that, as Christians, we have all been baptized into one body, the head or source of which is Jesus who nourishes it so it grows with a growth that is pleasing to God.[1]

It is also interesting to note that the words "head" and

"beginning" are used almost synonymously in reference to Christ in Paul's writings. Again, the idea which emerges is that of source, or something similar to our words "fountainhead" or "headwaters." Colossians 1:15-18 is a case in point. "He [that is, Jesus] is the image of the invisible God, the first-born of all creation. For by Him all things were created . . . all things have been created by Him and for Him. And He is before all things, and in Him all things hold together." Did you catch the feeling of source in that? "He is the *first*-born." "He is *before* all things." Then verse 18: "He is also head of the body, the church; and He is the beginning [here you have the two words, *head* and *beginning* almost side by side], the first-born from the dead; so that He Himself might come to have first place in everything." Here the emphasis subtly switches from function to position. That's why I am taking the time to deal so carefully with the duality of obvious agape love and unobvious authority, since both are involved in the principle of responsible headship.

Summing It Up

What does all this mean? What are the applications for you, my Christian brother? Simply this. As "house-band" God has given you the responsibility and equivalent authority to bind your household together. The band you use is love. Following the example of Jesus, you are to be head of your wife in the sense of being the source, the initiator, the instigator of self-humbling, self-giving ministry to your mate. And you, my sister, even as the church voluntarily responds to the loving actions initiated by Jesus, you are freed by your husband's Christlike attitude to respond to him voluntarily. Who is your example? Jesus.

Both male and female find their model in Him. As pattern for male, Jesus initiates continuing, unceasing, loving actions on behalf of His bride, the church. Whether He is responded to or not, He goes on initiating this kind of loving, caring action. If we fail to respond, we're the losers. But the instant we do respond, the moment we reciprocate and initiate a movement toward Him, as pattern for female, Jesus becomes responder. He humbly gives Himself to us in a most gracious and intimate way.

So Jesus is pattern for both husband and wife. He is initiator and responder. And He makes it clear by His own example that you don't have to stay locked into either one of these roles. As a husband you don't always have to be the loving initiator. As wife you are not limited to being the loving responder. Jesus demonstrates that you and your spouse are free to be one, or the other, or both. The prevailing atmosphere within your Christian marriage should be that of mutuality—reinforced with latent authority—laced with love.

One young man whom I recently joined in Christian marriage to a lovely girl put it this way: "I will usually be initiator, but will also be a responder. It is my desire to be sensitive to her needs and never lord it over her. I need to find her strengths and free her to use them effectively in our mutual submission." It couldn't be better said. Your example, my Christian brother, is provided by God your Father, Jesus your Savior, and the Holy Spirit your helper. This means your love is to be obvious, while your authority is to be latent. It must be active but not apparent, and rarely—if ever—arbitrary.

Laid-Back Authority in Marriage

When God's both/and answer is properly understood and applied, you and your mate will not "go around in circles of servile indecision," as someone has caricatured mutual submission. As we've seen, someone does have ultimate accountability *if it comes to that.* It is not a matter of hierarchy but stability. It has nothing to do with power but with protection of family unity from disorder.

The Principle of Responsible Headship as established by God is not legalistic or capricious or arbitrary. It has to do with caring. And commitment. And responsibility. *As long as there is a husband in a home, God wants him to accept the responsibility to be responsible and "preserve the unity of the Spirit in the bond of peace"* (Ephesians 4:3). This does not mean his wife can't or won't share that responsibility with him. In a mature, Spirit-controlled marriage in which mutuality is consistently lived out, she can and will! But if she doesn't, he must!

How he responds is the key. His goal should be decision by consensus—operational equality—the daily living out of Spirit-filled mutuality. But if there is a rare, rare, R-A-R-E moment in which there is not the time or opportunity or ability to reach a negotiated settlement—and he finds himself saying: "Someone must accept responsibility and I'm elected"—then that man must approach that moment in the spirit of self-giving, self-sacrificing love. If he manages it with a light touch rather than a heavy hand, the exceptional moment will be just that. Exceptional! If he becomes authoritarian rather than authoritative, the moment will lose its magic. It will deteriorate into carnal conflict. Sulking alienation. Or outright manipulation. And that's a tragedy.

To be sure it takes time and patience to arrive at a negotiated settlement. The point is, God wants you to opt, as He did, for effectiveness, not efficiency. Once you and your mate have settled the issue of "the bottom line" in keeping with God's concern for order you are ready to enjoy your freedom in expressing mutuality.

Granting Authority to Give Love

It may be a puzzlement at first as to how authority fits in with a husband's loving his wife as Christ loves the church. For instance, I don't need authority to love Lucille. At least not in principle! She's my wife and I'm commanded to love her. Loving her is both a responsibility and a joy. However, if my love is to be expressed in deeds, not just words—actually not theoretically—I must have authority in the form of her willingness to accept my love. She must authorize me, if you will, to love her. She must actualize my freedom to love her through a spirit of voluntary submission expressed in a willingness to be loved.

Now let's face it—this is an area where, to reverse the famous saying, the spirit is often *un*willing and the flesh is strong! But, wife, you must encourage your husband to love you as Christ loved the church. Sometimes it isn't easy for him to do so. It takes very little to quench the spirit in some men. Lack of encouragement can actually paralyze a man's willingness to initiate loving, caring acts for the benefit of his wife. So, wife, follow the counsel of Ephesians 5:22 and *voluntarily* submit to your husband *as to the Lord.* Allow the Christ in you to submit to the Christ in him in a way which honors and encourages the Principle of Responsible Headship on his part.

Suppose some morning your husband offers you the love gift of breakfast in bed. Not only does this announcement throw you into shock, but the mere thought of him pawing through your pots and pans in search of the eggbeater is clear cause for panic. He's a real kitchen klutz. Despite his good intentions, when he's finished fixing breakfast your neatly ordered kitchen will be a disaster area.

So you're faced with a choice. You can put a higher value on order in your kitchen, or on order in your relationship. At that particular moment, at least, you can't have both. So you voluntarily submit by granting him permission to love you in a way that represents a servant spirit by serving you breakfast in bed. The coffee may be so strong it would grow hair on a doorknob. The toast may look and taste like charcoal. The eggs may be as tough as rubber. But *he* took the risk of loving you in a way which was difficult if not downright dangerous, and because *you* put a higher value on order in your relationship than order in your kitchen, you freed him to become vulnerable again. And maybe—just maybe, with a bit of careful coaching on your part—while he never develops the skills of the galloping gourmet, his offer of breakfast in bed someday will produce pleasure instead of terror.

It comes down to this. Your husband's love of you is a measurable, tangible, attainable and manageable expression of his love of Jesus. By granting your partner permission to grow in his exercise of latent authority and thereby fulfill his responsibility to love you obviously just as Christ loved the church, you also free your mate to love Jesus more fully. When that happens your husband's love for you can't help but grow. And that's what *both* of you want, isn't it!

5

The Principle of Prevailing Atmosphere

If your marriage is to be truly Christian and thus all you desire it to be, the prevailing atmosphere in which you live out that relationship must be one of mutuality . . . reinforced with authority . . . laced with love. Ignorance of or indifference to God's both/and answer are precursors to anarchy with "everyone [doing] what [is] right in his own eyes" (Judges 21:25). A dreary way to live!

An aged couple who had achieved a beautiful one-flesh marriage became trapped in their automobile by a dead-end road. On one side was a steep wall. On the other a sharp precipice. The old gentleman cautiously tried to turn around, but one of the front wheels went over the edge. Knowing the danger, he asked his wife of some fifty years to get out while he sought to extricate the car. She answered softly, "No, dear, if you go, I want to go with you."

That's it, isn't it! To so live and love in mutual openness and vulnerability that being one in Christ is more important than life itself.

Mutual Submission as Prevailing Atmosphere

Just as Galatians 3:28 is the landmark text for the Principle of Equality with Diversity, so Ephesians 5:21 is your key to understanding the Principle of Prevailing Atmosphere: *Be subject to one another in the fear of [out of reverence for] Christ.*

The predominant environment in which all Christians are to live out *all* relationships is that of mutual submission. From the posture of brothers and sisters in Christ who joyfully acknowledge the Principle of Equality with Diversity and earnestly accept their common call to "preserve the unity of the Spirit in the bond of peace" (Ephesians 4:3), you and your partner are to build healthy, happy, attractive relationships in *every* area of your lives.

In Romans 2:10 Paul calls for Christians to outdo each other in showing honor. In Philippians 2:3 he urges you, in humility, to count others better than yourself. In both passages the principle is the same. As Christians, hungry for God's best in your relationships, you and your brothers and sisters in Christ are called upon to forsake the practices of a pagan world which attempts to dominate and lord it over others. Instead, you are to be submissive to one another, learning the spirit of submission through hard practice.

The concept of mutuality expressed in concern for, commitment to, and service of, the other person(s) in all relationships is articulated clearly in Colossians.

In Colossians 3:10-17 Paul explains how The Principle of Prevailing Atmosphere works out on a day-to-day basis.

Body Life: "... and have put on the new self who is being renewed to a true knowledge according to the image of the One who created him—a renewal in which there is no distinction between Greek and Jew, circumcised and uncircumcised, barbarian, Scythian, slave and freeman, but Christ is all, and in all. And so, as those who have been chosen of God, holy and beloved, put on a heart of compassion, kindness, humility, gentleness and patience; bearing with one another, and forgiving each other, whoever has a complaint against

73

anyone; just as the Lord forgave you, so also should you. And beyond all these things put on love, which is the perfect bond of unity. And let the peace of Christ rule in your hearts, to which indeed you were called in one body; and be thankful. Let the word of Christ richly dwell within you, with all wisdom teaching and admonishing one another with psalms and hymns and spiritual songs, singing with thankfulness in your hearts to God. And whatever you do in word or deed, do all in the name of the Lord Jesus, giving thanks through Him to God the Father."

In 3:18-19 he applies the principle to married life.

Married Life: "Wives, be subject to your husbands, as is fitting in the Lord. Husbands, love your wives, and do not be embittered against them."

In 3:20-21 to home life.

Home Life: "Children, be obedient to your parents in all things, for this is well-pleasing to the Lord. Fathers, do not exasperate your children, that they may not lose heart."

In 3:22—4:1 to vocational life.

Vocational Life: "Slaves, in all things obey those who are your masters on earth, not with external service, as those who merely please men, but with sincerity of heart, fearing the Lord. Whatever you do, do your work heartily, as for the Lord rather than for men; knowing that from the Lord you will receive the reward of the inheritance. It is the Lord Christ whom you serve. For he who does wrong will receive the consequences of the wrong which he has done, and that without

> partiality. Masters, grant to your slaves
> justice and fairness, knowing that you too
> have a Master in heaven."

A similar development is found in Ephesians 5:21 through 6:18, except—and this is most enlightening and encouraging—the Holy Spirit wisely inspired Paul to point out such extraordinary living is not possible in the flesh, but requires supernatural endowment. He reminds us in Ephesians 6:10 our strength must come from the Lord's mighty power which is within each Christian. There follows an inventory of the spiritual equipment God has prepared for those who are committed to reach for His best (Ephesians 6:11-17). The exhortation concludes: "With all prayer and petition pray at all times in the Spirit . . . with all perseverance and petition for all the saints" (Ephesians 6:18) . . . and that includes your mate!

In building a Christian marriage, you and your partner begin from the posture of brother and sister in Christ who are subject to one another out of reverence for Christ (Ephesians 5:21). This monumental text makes it clear *the prevailing atmosphere, in which* ALL *relationships between* ALL *Christians is to be lived out on a day-to-day basis, is that of mutual submission out of love, respect and reverence for the Christ in each of them.*

Why did the Holy Spirit call for submission rather than correction or education or continuing domination of one Christian by the other? The answer is simple—because of Jesus. Christ came, not to be ministered to, but to minister. Not to be served, but to serve. Out of reverence for the living example of Jesus, you and your mate—as brothers and sisters in Christ—are to learn submission to each other.

The pitfall into which many evangelicals have fallen in the past is the practice of picking Ephesians 5:21-33 apart so attention is focused on an individual phrase quoted in isolation rather than the central teaching of the section as a whole.

For instance, how many times have you heard the statement, "For the husband is the head of the wife" (verse 23a), lifted out of context and used as the starting point of an organizational chart for marriage and the home? When you look at the passage in its entirety, you discover the emphasis is not on control but on love.

This prompts a brief word to my Christian brothers: Your marriage license is not like the pink slip to your car. You do not own your wife, and you must not treat her like a possession. You are to love your wife and extend to her the same kind of self-giving, self-humbling service Jesus lavishes upon His church.

As we learned in the preceding chapter, being head, in the biblical sense, is the exact opposite of being commander-in-chief, chairman of the board, or president of the corporation. It requires a spirit of submissiveness expressed in obvious agape love and laid-back authority. It means happily and voluntarily ministering to your wife and her needs in precisely the same way Jesus is ever and always ministering to you—His bride—and your needs.

Get the Big Picture

To approach Ephesians 5:21-33 piecemeal is a grievous error. It must be seen as a single statement with a common theme throughout. When you approach it this way, you discover verse 21 is the landmark text which sets the tone for everything that follows. "Be subject to one another" is the central teaching here. The big picture. The idea Paul states clearly and without equivocation. It is the concept of mutual submission.

What comes after (verses 22-33) is an expansion upon that theme—an explanation of that great principle. It's as if Paul were saying, "Here is how the principle will work out for you, my sisters, and here is how it will work out for you, my brothers. Now, just to make sure you don't forget the principle, let me say it again in a slightly different way: 'nevertheless let each individual among you also love his own wife even as himself; and let the wife see to it that she respects her husband' " (verse 30).

Verse 21 said, "Submit to each other." Verse 33 says, "Love and respect each other." Both are saying the same thing: outdo each other in showing honor.

If you get hung up on the illustration Paul uses here and try to use it as a standard operating procedure for all people at all times in all situations, you'll miss the whole point of the teaching.

God's ideal for marriage is spelled out in Genesis 1 and 2. Anything less than that is a compromise on His ideal. All the laws and legalities scattered throughout scripture—including the concept of delegated authority—are God's loving accommodation to our fallen nature. They were never meant to be ironclad rules which make no allowance for the fact that, as Christians, you and your spouse have the incredible privilege, which non-Christians do not have, of entering the garden again, so to speak, where you can experience God's ideal and together, as man and wife, become one flesh in the full meaning of the term.

What It Means to Submit

Ephesians 5:21-33 sets forth the "flip side" of God's both/and answer, that is, the second basic condition which must be met if you and your spouse are to experience Christian marriage at its best. Laid-back authority is "side one." Mutual submission is "side two."

This may require that you set aside a lot of presuppositions regarding the word "submission." In all probability, much of what you have traditionally thought—or been taught—is not supported by scripture. So I ask you to devote your undivided attention to this next section. It may take you into unfamiliar territory.

For starters you need to know that in a patriarchal society such as that to which the book of Ephesians was originally written, it was not necessary to tell women to submit to their husbands. They had no choice but to submit or pay the consequences! This precipitated a great deal of cunning on the part of women as they learned to manipulate their husbands into being easier to live with. Conscious of this sociological reality, Paul taught Christian women to submit *in the right way. With the right spirit.* Since she had to submit anyway, let her do it *"as to the Lord"* (5:22). If she and her husband were both Christians the Christ in her was to honor the Christ in him. If she were a Christian and he was not, she was to submit to him out of reverence for Christ as the best of all means of winning him to Christ (I Peter 3:1-6). I have more to say about this in Chapter Nine.

As Christianity began to permeate social structures conditions changed. Today in a Christian marriage, *both* husband and wife are called upon to be active *co-partners* in building a relationship which is bossless. *Not* leaderless or headless, *bossless!* You are commanded by God to build a relationship which reflects the concept of "reciprocal superiority." That is, each of you—as equals—does that which you are best equipped to do, thereby participating in the mutual growth and fulfillment of you both.

Hurray for Hupotasso

If you are nervous about the possibility of our violating scripture when we suggest the Holy Spirit had something other than an organizational chart in mind when He inspired Paul to pen these words in Ephesians 5, let's look a bit deeper into scripture and see if there's any foundation for this fear.

I'm not a Greek scholar, but my knowledge of the language requires that I point out that chapter and verse numbering are not part of the original text. These were added by translators to facilitate our enjoyment and use of scripture. Furthermore, I must call your attention to the fact that in the Greek there is no verb in that section of the text we identify as verse 22. It is assumed from verse 21. If we had a direct translation the two verses would flow together and read as follows: "Submit to one another out of reverence for Christ, wives to your husbands." This means that any theology of Christian family based on a division of verses 21 and 22—assigning verse 21 to the church in general and verse 22 to the home—is weak at best. Verse 22 is rendered meaningless by this process, and a door is opened to misunderstanding the balance of what the Holy Spirit is teaching us here. The Greek language requires that sweet submission toward one another be the prevailing atmosphere maintained by both partners in a Christian home.

It is also of great importance that you know the word *hupotasso*, translated in Ephesians 5 as "submit" and "subject" is used in several forms throughout the New Testament. In its active form, it takes on the connotation of a military term and signifies an externally imposed submission based upon rank or position, and, in fact, emphasizes the rulership of Jesus.

Some of the passages in which *hupotasso* is used in this way are Romans 8:20, where twice the creation is described as being arbitrarily put into subjection, or I Corinthians 15:27, where three times God is said to have arbitrarily and externally put all things under His (Jesus') feet. Ephesians 1:22, Hebrews 2:5,8 and Philippians 3:21 also employ the active form of *hupotasso*, meaning externally imposed subjection of the lower by the higher.

But *hupotasso* has another form with a somewhat different spelling which is called the middle, or passive voice. In this form the verb switches from an externally imposed subjection—something which is arbitrarily done to you—

and becomes an internally initiated submission; that is, something you do voluntarily to yourself.

In English, we have a reasonable facsimile of this language difference in what are referred to as transitive and reflexive verbs. When a verb is transitive, the subject does something to the object. When the verb is reflexive, the subject does something to itself. These two forms of action, one externally imposed and the other internally initiated, are what we have described for us in the original Greek through the various voices of the verb *hupotasso*.

In I Corinthians 15:28 you find an interesting mixture of both forms in the same verse. In English the verb is virtually the same throughout. In Greek the first and the third clauses are in the active voice and refer to externally imposed subjection. The middle clause is in the passive voice describing how Jesus will voluntarily submit Himself so "God may be all in all." When all things are subjected [active voice] to Him, then the Son Himself also will be subjected [passive voice] to the One who subjected [active voice] all things to Him, that God may be all in all."

I know this has been a bit laborious, but we come now to what I call the "Sunday punch." In all marriage texts— Colossians 3, Ephesians 5, Titus 2 and I Peter 3—which reveal God's effort to show you a better way than the world's way of domination, the verb *hupotasso*, without exception, *is in the middle or passive voice!*

The submission to which you are called in your relationship as a Christian husband or wife is never, *ever*, something externally imposed! A demanding husband oppressing his wife. A domineering wife leading her husband around by the nose. Rather, your submission is to be an internalized response which springs naturally and voluntarily from your heart.

And notice, please, the submission is mutual. When you begin with Ephesians 5:21 and end with Ephesians 5:33, you see the argument makes full circle. In verse 21 you and your spouse are taught to submit to one another. In verse

33 you and your spouse are taught to love and respect one another.

To a Christian man living in a pagan world which thought—and often still thinks—of women as objects to be possessed or used, the Spirit of God says: "Love your wife. Voluntarily give her honor with respect."

To a Christian woman living in a pagan world which thought—and often still thinks—of men as adversaries to be cleverly manipulated, the Spirit of God says: "Respect your husband. Voluntarily give him honor with love."

It's a beautiful parallelism, you see, in which something is said to each of you which has deep meaning for both of you.

More on the Meaning of Submission

It should be clear by now that God had something truly special in mind when, through the reconciling work of Christ (II Corinthians 5:17-19), the Loving Father reopened the door to Perfect Marriage, that is, marriage as He meant it to be. Headship becomes servanthood. Submission becomes loving support and vulnerability.

This is pointed up when we consider the various definitions of our English word "submit." Any good dictionary will tell you "submit" means to yield or surrender to the power, control or authority of another. If you read on, however, you will find that "submit" also means to present or commit something for the consideration or judgment of another. For example, when a secretary submits the minutes of a previous meeting, he or she is laying out in an open manner a piece of supportive work for the inspection and acceptance of a responsible group. When you submit your income tax records to the IRS, you are presenting a very real part of yourself to the consideration and judgment of Uncle Sam.

Is it possible that one reason many people are soured on

submission is that they have overlooked this second, more subtle, but terribly significant meaning of the word? Consider the possibility that when the Holy Spirit instructs you to "submit to one another" (Ephesians 5:21) He is exhorting you to voluntarily be open to, vulnerable with and supportive of each other. Instead of demanding that you surrender to the power, control or authority of your mate, the exciting challenge is to open yourself up to the possibility of really being known and hence understood and lovingly supported by your mate. Risky? You bet! Unless—help me, Lord, to make that word as big as it really is—UNLESS the risk is tempered by love. Then it is no risk at all. It is high adventure full of dynamic discoveries and the joy of knowing and being known, accepting and being accepted, supporting and being supported.

In the preceding chapter we learned a Christian husband is challenged to change from a control mentality toward one which reveals deep caring for his wife. He is to *agape* her (Ephesians 5:25). The book of Titus adds the electrifying news that a Christian wife is to view her husband as a friend rather than an adversary. She is to *phileo* him (Titus 2:3-4).

In the Bible *phileo* is that remarkable quality of love one feels for a cherished friend of either sex. Jesus felt *phileo* for one of his disciples (John 13:23). The Heavenly Father has *phileo* for His only begotten Son (John 5:20a). *Phileo* is friendship love of the highest order.

For a first-century Christian wife to be told she was to *phileo*—be best friend to—her husband was revolutionary. It was as demanding of her as Calvary love was of him. One thing a first-century husband and wife were not was friends! Everything in that restrictive society militated against the intensity and joy of such fondness. To be sure, there were exceptions, but holding each other dear, cherishing, multifaceted comradeship and rapport were rare in first-century homes.

They are almost as hard to come by today. The competitive context in which many modern marriages are lived out discourages a wife from viewing her husband as a friend. But the biblical injunction remains. *Cherish is God's word for you, my Christian sister.* Cherish your husband. Build rapport with him. Enrich your relationship through attitudes and activities which foster friendship. Develop comradeship with him. Treat him tenderly. Hold him dear. *Phileo* him!

The balance, fairness and revolutionary equality in God's equation for Perfect Marriage begins to come into focus. For the husband headship becomes servanthood. For the wife submission becomes loving support. For both husband and wife, voluntary vulnerability becomes the order of the day—the prevailing atmosphere—in which they live out their love for each other.

A Christian husband is to *agape* his wife. A Christian wife is to *phileo* her husband. Each is instructed—and equipped by the Holy Spirit—to enter the high adventure of mutual openness. And how sweet it is—this mutuality of knowing and being known, of understanding and being understood, of supporting and being supported—how sweet indeed!

Could we expect the loving Father to have planned it otherwise? Of course not. Submission as voluntary loving support represents His best. It puts flesh on The Principle of Prevailing Atmosphere. Mutuality ceases to be a fond ideal and becomes a fervent passion. In this manner the stage is set for negotiating happy solutions to the issues of who leads and when, who decides and what, who works and where.

Some Implications of Mutual Submission

Our strategy in this volume has been somewhat different from the typical "how to" book on marriage (how to solve this problem; how to resolve that situation). As a matter of fact, I haven't given you any specific answers to any specific questions. Nor is it my plan to. Instead, our emphasis throughout is on biblical principles for a very simple reason. If you learn an answer, you can respond to a question. If you master a principle, you can solve all kinds of questions. In fact, it is my contention that if you and your mate master and are mastered by the biblical principles for Christian marriage discussed in this book, there aren't any problems or situations within that relationship which the two of you can't work out together.

As Genesis 3:16 explains, the fall of man radically altered what we might call the balance of power between male and female. The equality with diversity which God designed into the human race was upset. The ability of Adam and Eve to function as equal partners in their relationship was seriously impaired. To help bring order out of chaos which followed the fall of man, God established a system of delegated authority designed to keep mankind from destroying itself.

In addition, when God sent His Son into the world, He had a lot more in mind than many of us have ever realized. For now, by the grace of the Lord Jesus who came to right all the relationships sin had made wrong, you and your mate, if you're Spirit-filled Christians, can actually enter Eden again, so to speak, where together the two of you can begin the high adventure of discovering and experiencing God's ideal for marriage.

When you begin to explore the wonder of what that means, you learn, among other things, that marriage as God meant it to be is one in which both partners maintain a proper relationship with God, allowing Him to do for them what only God can do. This frees them to do for each other that which only they can do.

Since Jesus is model for both husband and wife, by His example Jesus makes it clear that there are no sexual stereotypes into which men and women are irrevocably locked. The man doesn't *always* have to be loving initiator.

The woman doesn't *always* have to be loving responder. Instead, guided by the Holy Spirit, you and your mate are free to be one, or the other, or both as the situation or need requires.

This kind of bossless Christian marriage doesn't just happen. It requires work. Lots of it! In fact, if I were to define Christian marriage in a single word, it would be "work." If I were to define it in two words, it would be "hard work." But the biblical ideal is a relationship in which each of you share an equal and mutual desire to glorify God by ministering to the other.

Therefore, how about making a decision to credit each other with *wanting* and *trying* to be all God wants you to be in this relationship? Then, if you, as wife, ask: "Is *that* how Christ loves?" and the answer is a resounding "No!" or you, as husband, ask: "Is *that* voluntary submission?" and again the answer is "No," both of you will automatically give each other a passing grade for *trying* and an "A" for *wanting* to try! It seems to me this would remove so much of the judgmentalism which worms its way into Christian homes and would build an attitude of acceptance of the humanity in your partner which sometimes results in him or her missing the mark. No Spirit-led Christian *wants* to miss the mark, and that's my point.

Marriage is on-the-job training of the severest sort. But if you and your mate are prepared to work at it, you can develop a lifestyle which results in a thoroughly biblical, wonderfully practical and absolutely delightful way of leading, deciding and working together. This will not only enrich the two of you, but bless the lives of all with whom you come in contact day by day.

Leading

How does the Principle of Prevailing Atmosphere work out in the routine, but practical and important, areas of leading, deciding and working? Well, let's start with leading, because who leads and how is basic.

Someone has said: "Christian marriage is a two-way street without a dividing line down the middle." This means you and your mate must approach the issue of leading prayerfully, carefully and with full knowledge that leading and being head are not the same. Being head is one aspect of leading, but submission is a form of leading, too. In the perfect marriage you and your mate are working toward, both of you are called upon to be active co-partners in building a relationship which is bossless. A relationship which reflects the concept of what John Stuart Mill calls "reciprocal superiority." Then each of you can enjoy the luxury of looking up to the other and can have, alternately, the pleasure of leading and of being led along the path toward true self-realization in Jesus.

A bossless Christian marriage is not leaderless. It is an equalitarian relationship in which you and your partner not only voluntarily submit to being led at times, but also take the necessary risks and responsibilities of leading at other times. As leadership oscillates between the two of you, each of you is free to do that which he or she does best for mutual growth and development.

In a bossless Christian marriage, leadership should and will float to the partner best equipped by God to function as leader in that place at that time. Or to say it another way, in Christian marriage, leadership is a contract which is constantly being renegotiated as both of you learn to say such things as, "If it's okay with you, I'll take care of that." Or, "You do this, honey; you're better at it than I am."

These statements aren't made to gain power on one hand or to escape responsibility on the other. They are said because they just plain make sense and express the joint commitment of you and your mate to a style of leading which is really helping and serving at its best. It is leading which liberates, fulfills and moves both of you toward maturity in Christ.

A Christian marriage is one in which leadership is not and should not be a static state, but something fluid. Something which, by deliberate choice, flows back and forth from one to the other based upon mutual esteem, wise use of your natural talents and keen sensitivity to your spiritual gift.[1]

This concept of oscillating leadership rests upon mutual submission. There can be no leadership without a willingness to be led. If you do not allow your mate to lead when he or she is best qualified by God to do so, you not only deprive yourself of a great blessing, but you also cheat your mate of a chance to develop his or her full potential and personhood. Truly there is wisdom in the admonition: "Be subject to one another out of reverence to Christ."

Deciding

A second area in which the Principle of Prevailing Atmosphere expressed in loving support has important implications is that of deciding. There are three key words which apply to the process of deciding in a bossless Christian marriage. They are: cooperation, alternation (not altercation!) and differentiation.

Cooperation refers to joint action taken by both of you working together in harmony at a given time. Alternation is that process in which one of you, with the full approval and support of the other, makes decisions at certain times because it makes sense to do so, while the other makes decisions at other times for the same reason and with the same strong feeling of support and approval. Differentiation means dividing up the decision-making process according to abilities, interests and spiritual gifts.

Whether these three modes of deciding are worked separately or together, they'll help you and your mate grow together rather than apart, because life will no longer be limited to rigidly marked areas of authority labeled "his" or "hers." By practicing mutual submission in decision-making, you silence the loud word "me" and accentuate the proud word "we." This can only be done as it should be done through the power of the Holy Spirit who enables you to love as Jesus loves.

When it comes to deciding, the big issue in Christian marriage is not *who* is right, you or your mate, but *what* is right. That calls for clear understanding which, in turn, requires careful communication. More about that in Chapter Eight.

The most helpful suggestion I can make right now is that you resist the temptation to make decisions right now! In other words, slow down the pace of your decision-making process. One of the problems we face today is the pressure to do and/or decide everything *right now*. This totally ignores the varying tempos people naturally follow in making changes and adjustments.

Some folk are imperative. They have a "let's get the show on the road" type temperament. Others are deliberative. They require more time to make up their minds. Their first response to almost everything is "no." As a result, they may come off sounding negative. They aren't. They are merely deliberative and saying "no" is a way of buying time to think through the decision they are being asked to make.

A friend of mine explained this natural difference in decision-making tempo to a woman who had come to him for counseling. When he finished, she said, "That explains it! For years my husband would come home from work and when I'd ask him to go to a movie after dinner he'd say 'no,' but thirty minutes later he'd be out in the driveway honking the horn, urging me to hurry up or we'd miss the show. I thought he was nuts! Now I know he is only deliberative."

Other folk are adaptive. They bend like a willow. Whatever the crowd wants to do, wherever their mate wants to go, is just fine with them. They may appear spineless or wishy-washy. They aren't. They usually have very deep convictions. They are just adaptive and are quite willing to let other people make most of the decisions.

If you put various combinations of these people together in a marriage, you're going to have problems unless you resist the "let's get this issue decided *right now*" philosophy. Therefore, one of the most helpful things you can do to settle the dust, as far as decision-making goes, is to slow down the pace so not only the decision, but the way you make it, will be glorifying to Jesus, the silent listener to every conversation in your Christian home.

Do I make it sound easy? It isn't. But the achievements of this kind of bossless marriage and home are cumulative. As the old gospel hymn puts it, "Each victory will help you some other to win." If you and your partner will persevere; if you can grasp the good news that Jesus died to save you from all sin, including the sin of relationships which Satan has turned sour; if you genuinely believe God's ideal for you is better than any of the traditional stereotypes He has permitted as an accommodation to man's fallen nature; if you accept the fact that in Christ you are one, that in Jesus there is neither male nor female; and if together, you commit yourselves earnestly and willingly to experiencing God's best in your marriage and home; you shall! God never gives you a dream of better things without also providing the grace you need to achieve it.

Working

The concept of mutual submission requires flexibility in all things. Your division of labor is no exception. This means you and your mate may need to re-examine the traditional line of demarcation between "women's" work and "men's" work.

When you look to scripture for guidance in this regard, you discover that what is so often thought of as a God-ordained division of labor occurred *after* the fall. Prior to that time, Adam and Eve were both given responsibility for parenting and fulfilling what someone has called their "cultural mandate."

"And God blessed them; and God said to them, 'Be fruitful and multiply [fulfill your mutual responsibility as parents], and fill the earth, and subdue it; and rule over the fish of the sea and over the birds of the sky, and over every living thing that moves on the earth [fulfill your mutual responsibility for planet earth]' " (Genesis 1:28).

You can't read that text and conclude it was God's intention there be separate spheres and different functions designated for husband and wife. In God's ideal for marriage, both Adam and Eve were equally responsible before Him for every aspect of life on this globe.

While there are obvious instructions given throughout both the Old and New Testaments, these are accommodations to the problem inherent in man's fallen nature. God's *ideal* for marriage, as spelled out in Genesis 1 and 2, is clearly that of interchangeable roles. As Christians desiring God's best for your marriage, you and your mate can and should fulfill a variety of functions as needs, circumstances, natural talents and spiritual gifts demand.

Again, it won't be easy. As Spirit-filled Christians, you and your mate have the incredible possibility, which non-Christians do not have, of experiencing God's ideal for marriage. With that as a real possibility, it would be a tragedy if you settled for anything less!

To be sure, there's the old carnal nature to deal with, and Satan, your adversary, will use it if he can to keep you from enjoying God's best. Someone once said the biggest adjustment a young wife has to make upon getting married is getting used to being whistled for instead of whistled at!

Well, it doesn't have to be that way. If Jesus could pick

up a towel and wash the disciples' feet, why can't a Christian husband emulate the love of Jesus by picking up a cloth and dusting the furniture? If a godly woman could learn to wisely handle the family resources as did the much-prized woman in Proverbs 31, why can't a Christian wife be trusted to manage the family budget? It may only be a convenience now, but with most wives outliving their husbands by five to ten years, it could be an absolute necessity in the future.

Some time ago, a young couple made an appointment for premarital counseling. In the course of our visit the young man shared how, because he worked rather late and his fiancee enjoyed preparing his dinner, he would help her with the dishes.

"My dad says, 'You're ruining her. That's woman's work.'" He paused, looked at me wistfully and said, "Pastor, is my dad right, or is what I feel in my heart right? I like to go out in the kitchen and help her with the dishes. It gives us a chance to be together and share things which have happened while we've been apart throughout the day."

"Great!" I said. "Do it. In the process, remember Jesus who exercised His headship and demonstrated His manhood by serving instead of being served."

A kindergarten teacher asked a new arrival what her father's name was. "Daddy," replied the little girl.

"No, I mean his first name. What does your mother call him?"

"Oh, she doesn't call him anything," was the child's reply. "She likes him."

I don't think it could be said any better, do you? A Christian marriage is that blessed relationship which enables both of you to grow in Christ as, through the power of the Holy Spirit, you learn to exhibit the fruit of the Spirit—love.

6

The Principle of Diversity With Unity

"Then God said, 'Let us make man in our image, according to our likeness'... And God created man in His own image, in the image of God He created him; *male and female* He created them" (Genesis 1:26,27, italics added for emphasis). Wouldn't you think an all-wise creator would have known better than to do that! Surely God must have foreseen the perversity to which such diversity was subject and could have found some other way to carry on the human race.

Zoology has a few happy examples of critters which are neither masculine nor feminine. They're both. Couldn't God have created a human "it," or "they," or "whatcha-macallit" which could keep the race going and, like the oyster, lead what Ogden Nash described as "a soothing kind of life"?[1]

Obviously He could have, but He didn't. And in its beginning pages, the Bible describes how God elected to make mankind in the form of individuals of two different sorts so they might meet, love, marry and minister to each other. Having done so, we're told God looked at what He had made and called it "very good" (Genesis 1:31).

This leads us to an important conclusion: Though you and your mate may have problems to solve in building a stable Christian marriage—and though at times it must seem as if nature itself is against you—diversity is not the culprit, *per*versity is. God called His creation of male and female good. So the fact you're different isn't the problem. Sin is!

Part of the Good News is that, through Jesus and the power of His resurrection, you and your mate, as Spirit-filled Christians, can overcome sin. You can conquer destructive habits. And believe it or not, *because* of your diversity (not in spite of it) you and your spouse can begin to experience the excitement and exhilaration of marriage as God meant it to be.

As we discovered through exposure to The Principle of Equality With Diversity, the concepts of superiority and inferiority have no place in a Christian marriage. As two of the Father's children eager for His best, you live together in racial, relational and responsible equality. But to speak of you and your mate as equals is to tell only half the truth. There is also the factor of diversity to contend with. God did not create a unisex, but human beings of two different kinds. "Male and female He created them" (Genesis 1:27).

What was His purpose in doing so? Did He intend this diversity to produce the perplexity, polarity and perversity as we see in so many marriages today? Or did God have something else in mind? My study of scripture leads me to say: *The good Lord never meant maleness or femaleness to subvert humanness. Diversity is a healthy antidote to dullness, but it was never meant to divide. God's intention for His children is that they live together in unity.*

Look again at scripture: "Male and female He created them . . . For this cause a man shall leave his father and his mother, and shall cleave to his wife; and they shall become one flesh" (Genesis 1:27; 2:24). There you have it—etched indelibly for all to see—The Principle of Diversity With Unity.

"Male and female He created them." In their unlikeness, their difference, their multiformity Adam and Eve were in a state of diversity. But, it was diversity with unity. They were one flesh. Plural means: consisting of or equal to more than one. But in their connectedness Adam and Eve were without plurality. While they were not the same, they were *one.*

This is God's ideal for you and your mate. It is His intention that you come to understand and enjoy the diversity which by deliberate design, He built into your humanity. It is not God's intention that you allow this diversity to destroy your unity.

Sexual Stereotypes Are Not Biblical

When we speak from a strictly biblical perspective, the most we can say with absolute certainty is that there are differences between male and female. Beyond that there is little we can say with finality, for the Bible is strangely silent when it comes to the exact nature of those differences. There are plenty of cultural and traditional stereotypes which, in ignorance, Christians have sometimes supported or even encouraged.

But when we set aside our presuppositions, pick up the Bible and allow it to speak for itself, we discover, to the dismay of some and the shame of others, that the scripture simply does not support the sexual stereotypes many have taken for granted and sometimes even thought were God ordained.

A few years ago a mental health survey was conducted by two competent professionals. Their findings were as follows: according to the average person on the street, the "mentally healthy male" is aggressive, independent, unemotional, logical, direct, adventurous, self-confident and ambitious. On the other hand, the "mentally healthy female" is thought to be passive, emotional, dependent, less competitive, non-objective, submissive, vain, easily influenced, religious and in need of security.[2]

In some instances, their assessments may be accurate, but this is definitely not the way God meant it to be. These stereotypes are cultural, not biblical. This is the way the world thinks. Sometimes, in ignorance of what the Bible really says, it is the way Christians think. However, if you take a careful look at scripture, these popular generalizations will be blown out of the water.

The Bible presents an impressive array of distinguished women who demonstrated all the positive qualities and characteristics attributed to both sexes. In the process, they accomplished tremendous things in a wide variety of fields. They failed at fitting a stereotype, but they excelled at being human!

As you survey the prominence, abilities, accomplishments and positive characteristics of the people, male and female, whom Holy Writ records as seeking God's best for their lives and their loved ones, a powerful truth should begin to seep through: It isn't God's will for you and your mate to rebel against the diversity which exists between you, it is His will that you revel in it. He loves for you to live together in harmony as you practice The Principle of Diversity With Unity. It is His desire that you learn to be what you are, allow your mate to be what he or she is and, in the process, discover what it means to be one.

Relish Your Diversity

God's ideal is that you and your mate relish your diversity without perplexity. To relish something is to be pleased with or by it. In a well-planned meal, the relish is that which renders the rest of the food more palatable and stimulating. Similarly, when God put you and your mate together as male and female, He meant for you to be pleased by your diversity rather than perplexed by it. Admittedly, that's sometimes hard to do.

A friend of mine who has three lovely married daughters shared the trauma he experienced each time he walked one of those lithe, little misses down the aisle. "John," he told me, "it was like giving a Stradivarius to a gorilla."

There *are* certain differences between the sexes, but

these need not be a source of anxiety. God designed the physiological differences and called them good. All you need to do is understand them so they work for you rather than against you. Instead of defining and exploring these biological factors, the Bible simply says—God made you male and female. It then proceeds to affirm your equality and unity, stressing similarities rather than diversities. Therefore, to understand your *biological* differences and any behavioral effects these differences may have, we must turn to extra-biblical sources.

Among the interesting things medical textbooks explain is that, of the 46 chromosomes in every fertilized egg, only two have anything to do with sexuality. The other 44 simply constitute a human being. If the two remaining chromosomes are XY, a male is on the way. If they are XX, a female will be born.

Another interesting fact is that everyone, man or woman, has a certain amount of both endrogen, the male hormone, and estrogen, the female hormone. As a result, as you might expect, there is no such thing as a purely masculine or totally feminine person. All of us are an intricate mixture of both. Therefore, from a scientific as well as biblical perspective, it really isn't possible to say there are certain traits which are feminine and others which are masculine. There are diversities, to be sure, but they are diversities which make you special, which give you individuality and distinction.

Inherent in your personhood is the fact that you are a unique combination of those qualities which are not male or female, but human. For instance, there are optimists and pessimists. There are introverts and extroverts. There are cycloids—folk who are most content in a structured environment—and there are schizoids—people who are happiest in an unstructured atmosphere. There are feeling-thinkers, and there are thinking-feelers. There are initiators and responders. There are people who are imperative, others who are deliberative, and still others who are adaptive. There are folk who are tough and others who are tender. To top it off, there are the factors of heredity and environment which affect us all.

When you think specifically of God's children, as differentiated from non-Christians, you discover there is not only an incredible variety in terms of natural talents and personality traits, but also a diversity of spiritual gifts accompanied by both a carnal and a spiritual nature.

However, none of these is sexual in origin. And that's the point! You and your mate may be any two of an infinite number of arrangements of these components, but they have nothing to do with your gender. They are not related in any way to maleness or femaleness, but to humanness.

Which leads us back to the *one* thing we can say with certainty based upon scripture: There are differences between male and female—God did not create a unisex—but the differences are physiological, period. All other supposed signs of maleness or femaleness are cultural and traditional in origin. Either that, or they are God's loving accommodations to our fallen nature and were never meant to be ends in themselves, but are means to the end that we might ultimately become like Jesus who is model for both male and female.

For instance, take the roles of initiator and responder spelled out in Ephesians 5. Do these represent God's ideal? Is it His intention that men and women be frozen into these roles so man is always required to be initiator and woman responder? Or are these ministries to one another really God's accommodation to the residual effects of our fallen nature just as the cross was His accommodation to our lostness?

It was not God's intention that Adam and Eve sin, but when they did, He had a plan—laid before the foundation of the world, the Bible says (Ephesians 1:4)—to deal with their rebellion through the crucifixion of His Son. It occurs to me that, even as the cross represents God's response to the circumstances caused by sin, so too, the roles of initiator and responder are His accommodation to the lingering effects of our Adamic nature. They do not represent God's best. They are the starting place where, as Christians, you and your spouse must begin to methodically build a relationship which *does* mirror God's ideal because both of you are free to initiate or respond in love as your needs, talents, circumstances and spiritual gifts demand.

So I repeat: the one thing we can say with absolute certainty, based upon scripture, is that there are differences between male and female—God did not create a unisex—but the differences are physiological, period.

A Little Leaguer approached a fellow player at practice. "How come you throw like a girl?" he asked.

"Because I am a girl," was the response. "So what!"

Good answer. God wants you to relish your diversity without perplexity. He wants you to accept it as a fact of life. There are certain physiological differences between male and female. There are differences in tissue, skeletal structure, metabolism, muscular formation, even blood content.

Typically, a woman's blood contains more water and about 20 percent fewer red cells. Since the red cells supply oxygen to the body, she tires more easily and is more prone to faint. On an average, her heartbeat tends to be more rapid and her blood pressure somewhat lower than the typical male. She carries an extra layer of fatty tissue—probably to facilitate her role as a walking incubator during pregnancy—and, while it's true that in terms of brute strength men are 50 percent stronger than women on an average, it is actuarially proven, in the United States at least, that women outlive men by several years.

The point is: What difference do all these differences make? Why should you and your mate be stereotyped and consigned to various roles simply on the basis of sex? You are not animals controlled by instinct. You have a higher heredity. You are made in the image of God. Both of you. Male and female! Instead of resisting your differences or making a great mystery out of them, you should learn to relish your diversity without perplexity because it was God's idea.

Along with her role in reproduction, there is, of course, the distinctly feminine function of menstruation. The evidence is clear that significant glandular and hormonal changes occur during the menstrual cycle which, in turn, affect how she feels and responds to life situations. However, there is strong evidence that men have a monthly cycle, too.

Did you know that approximately every 26 days a man goes through physiological changes which are often accompanied by definite mood swings? I told that to one woman and she said, "Nonsense! My husband is very even tempered—mad all the time!"

It's also a known fact that men, as well as women, eventually go through a change of life when their hormonal balance shifts, sometimes with very distressing symptoms, including a decline in sexual prowess, if not interest.

Along with medical assistance available for both men and women during this time of life, there is, for the Christian, the ministry of the Holy Spirit. I am personally acquainted with any number of people, men and women, who have learned to master their moods rather than be mastered by them. With effective hormone therapy supported by love, understanding, compassion, patience and moment-by-moment dependence on the Holy Spirit, women, who by their own testimony used to be once-a-month witches; and men, who by their own admission used to cater to their unexpected mood swings rather than control them, are now managing themselves better.

Furthermore, they are voluntarily reaching out to support their mate during times of oppression. In the process, they are learning to relish their diversity without perplexity as they minister to each other in those ways which are their unique and special privilege as life partners.

Respect Your Diversity

A second powerful application of The Principle of Diversity With Unity requires that you and your mate respect your diversity without polarity. Polarity is a very interesting word. It means: a state of moving or being apart. It refers to positions, roles and attitudes which are fixed— literally poles apart.

In Christian marriage, however, there is no place for polarity. By virtue of being new creatures in Christ, you and your mate are put back in the garden, so to speak, where you can discover and experience God's ideal.

What do you find in Eden? You discover God made male and female long before the fall. Now that's important. It means that whether Adam and Eve had or had not sinned, diversity was part of God's plan. It was the way He meant it to be. If these physiological differences are creation-deep as the Genesis account clearly indicates, then there's something in the nature of you and your mate which fits together and enables you to complement each other. But that can't happen unless you respect your diversity without polarity. If you allow your differences to divide you, you'll miss God's best, for the goal set in Genesis 2:24 is that you two become one flesh.

To do that will require that you really work at deepening your awareness of and commitment to the friendship which exists between you. Though radically different from each other, the two of you may enjoy the closest friendship for a lifetime. It is not a requisite of friendship that both participants be alike in all things. It is enough that you be alike at the points where your hearts touch. As A. W. Tozer has said, "Harmony is likeness at points of contact. Friendship is likeness where hearts merge."[3]

A four-year-old, observing his mom and dad hug each other in the kitchen one evening, explained, "Hey, there's no room between you!" In a simple way the youngster's observation expresses a profound truth. When you and your mate learn to cleave to each other in the sense of actively responding to the needs of the other, there won't be room for things to come between you.

Now a healthy cleaving doesn't mean the two of you become clinging vines. On the contrary, Christian marriage is something far more intimate than the neurotic dependence of people who desperately need each other for the sake of emotional or spiritual survival.

Need and love are very close, but they are not the same. That's why it's imperative for your Christian marriage to be built on The Principle of Fullness Before Overflow. As two whole persons, each of whom is involved in a uniquely personal, intimate, loving relationship with God Himself, you will sense that, if necessary, you could make it alone with a full feeling of personhood. Nevertheless, you choose to be married to each other in order that you might experience God's best *for both of you.* Therefore, neither of you find your diversity threatening. You find it thrilling!

You and your mate are not the same because people are not the same. God has never yet made two human beings exactly alike. As a result, there will be significant differences between you and your life partner. God wants you to handle this diversity without polarity—without resorting to the cultural stereotypes which have grown up over the centuries. "What can you expect from a man!" "Just like a woman!"

The Lord Jesus bridged all stereotypes and brought together in His person those qualities and characteristics of people as God meant people to be. He was initiator. He was responder. He was thinker. He was feeler. He was tender. He was tough. He personified those attributes which are traditionally called masculine and expressed those qualities which are thought to be feminine. He refused to conform to cultural sex roles. He never felt compelled to prove His masculinity by throwing His weight around, yet He was strong in the face of temptation and

101

courageous when confronted with hostility. His logic confounded many and His demands for justice were unswerving. Yet, He was tender and loving, gentle and meek.

In every way Jesus was a worthy example for both you and your mate. He demonstrated in His person and in His relationships the possibility of respecting diversity without polarity. And, if the two of you will invite Jesus to express Himself in your relationship, you'll come to see that in a Christian marriage certain words just don't apply. Words like: impossible, never, separation, divorce.

The goal you have set for yourself is marriage-long. It requires that as long as you live you never stop working at the hard, rewarding task of becoming one flesh, of respecting your diversity without polarity.

Revel in Your Diversity

Last, but not least, it is God's desire that you and your mate learn to revel in your diversity without perversity. Considering your status as sinners saved by grace—but sinners, nonetheless—I think it's only fair to say, this too is hard to do, because the old carnal nature is very perverse.

Some years ago there was an article in the *Saturday Evening Post* which illustrates this point quite well. It was called, "The Seven Ages of the Married Cold." When his wife came down with a cold during the first year of their marriage, the husband said, "Sugar dumpling, I'm worried about my baby girl. You've got a bad sniffle and there's no telling about those things with all this strep going around. I'm putting you in the hospital this afternoon for a general checkup and a good rest. I know the food's lousy, but I'll bring your meals in from Rossini's. I've already got it arranged with the floor superintendent."

When she came down with a cold during the second year they were married, he said, "Listen, darling, I don't like the sound of that cough and I've called Doc Miller to rush over here. Now you go to bed like a good girl, please? Just for papa.''

When the third year rolled around and she got a cold, he said, "Maybe you'd better lie down, honey; nothing like a little rest when you feel punk. I'll bring you something to eat. Have we got any soup?"

And then there was the fourth year. "Look, dear, be sensible. After you feed the kids and get the dishes washed, you'd better hit the sack."

By the fifth year he was saying, "Why don't you get yourself a couple of aspirin?"

When she came down with a cold during the sixth year of marriage, he said, "If you'd just gargle or something, instead of sitting around barking like a seal!"

And finally, in the seventh year he was heard to say, "For Pete's sake, stop sneezing! Whatcha trying to do, gimme pneumonia?"[6]

I read about a chap who commented, "I wouldn't say my wife always gets her own way, but she does write out her diary a week ahead!"

Indeed, the residual effects of our fallen nature give all of us a tussle at times. But it doesn't have to be that way. It is possible for you and your mate to really enjoy your diversity without perversity. It's possible, through the power of the Holy Spirit, to be as Adam and Eve were before the fall—physically different, but spiritually one— and therefore soul mates in the sense that the way each of them thought, felt and decided fortified the other.

It's true, sin spoiled all that and, as a result of their disobedience, Adam and Eve died spiritually. No longer one in the truest sense, they lost their ability to function effectively as soul mates. Instead of being controlled by the Holy Spirit, their souls—mind, emotions and will—were dominated by the flesh. The Bible graphically describes the perplexity, polarity and perversity which resulted.

But, praise God, through the person of the Lord Jesus, it

is possible for you and your mate to experience God's ideal again. *Like* Adam and Eve, the two of you are tripartite beings: body, soul and spirit.

Unlike Adam and Eve who never regained spiritual life, when you were born again you became spiritually alive. Your soul—that thinking, feeling, deciding part of you—was also saved. That is to say: your mind or the way you think, your emotions or the way you feel, your will or the way you decide were redeemed and freed to function creatively. When you and your spouse are filled with the Holy Spirit you actually become soul mates again, so your corporate thoughts, emotions and will reflect the character of Jesus who is model for you both.

Your body remains the same although, as I have said, great things can happen even there to smooth out the valleys and peaks created by hormonal imbalance and other physiological factors. However, for the most part, you and your mate will rejoice in the physical diversities which set you apart as male and female. In the area of body, there probably isn't much you'd *want* to change.

But in the area of spirit—oh!—fantastic things can happen. As you and your mate allow God's Holy Spirit to fill your human spirit and as this begins to affect your thinking, feeling, and deciding, you will be soul mates in the happiest sense of the word—able to experience diversity without perversity. Therefore, may I urge you ever so earnestly: If you really want to do something for your marriage, be filled with the Holy Spirit! That is, deliberately, consciously and willingly place yourself under the domination and control of the Holy Spirit. Scripture describes people who are filled with many things: anger, fear, greed, lust. These people were controlled or dominated by these negative emotions. Scripture directs us to "be filled with the Holy Spirit" (Ephesians 5:18), and I take that to mean we are to choose domination and control by God's best rather than our worst.

Have you ever noticed that the admonition to be filled

comes immediately prior to Paul's instruction regarding Christian marriage? "Be filled with the Spirit" (Ephesians 5:18). Ephesians 5:21, three verses later, says, "Be subject to one another . . ." Do you suppose the Holy Spirit inspired Paul to put it in that order because God knew you and your mate couldn't be mutually loving, open, vulnerable and supportive without His help?

I repeat, if you really want to do something for your marriage, be filled with the Holy Spirit.

Harmony in marriage is not becoming alike. Harmony in marriage is you and your spouse joyfully accepting and freely delighting in each other—*as you are*—when filled with the Holy Spirit. For it's He, the paraclete, the ultimate helper, who makes you like Jesus and thus liberates your potentialities as persons. Not as male or female, but as human beings made in the image of God.

Do I make it sound easy? It isn't. It calls for hard work, discipline and commitment on the part of you both. But God's ideal is that you and your spouse really enjoy The Principle of Diversity With Unity. Christian marriage is that marvelous amalgamation in which one times one equals one. Hard? Yes! Tough? You bet! Impossible? Never! You are not asked to do it alone. You are invited to do it together—with God.

When George Mallory and a party of Englishmen attempted to scale Mount Everest, they were foiled in their historic attempt after climbing to a height of over 25,000 feet. One of the team returned to England to tell their story and was invited to speak to a large London audience. Part of his presentation included a huge, blown-up photograph of Mount Everest. After describing the difficulties and tragedies of their expedition, the man turned and addressed the mountain.

"Everest," he said, "we tried to conquer you once, but you overpowered us. We tried to conquer you a second time, and again, you were too much for us. But, Everest, I want you to know we're going to conquer you, for you can't grow any bigger, but we can!''

That's the glory of the Christian life. That's the spirit in which you and your mate can conquer. The difficulties you face may be many, but they aren't infinite. Your capacity to grow, is! So, if together you grow with God, there are no limits to how far or how high the three of you can go!

7

The Principle of Sexuality

"Then God said, 'Let us make man in our image, according to our likeness'...And God created man in His own image, in the image of God He created him; male and female He created them. And God blessed them; and God said to them, 'Be fruitful and multiply, and fill the earth and subdue it'...And the man and his wife were both naked and were not ashamed...Now the man had relations with his wife Eve, and she conceived and gave birth to Cain, and she said, 'I have gotten a manchild with the help of the Lord'" (Genesis 1:26,27; 2:25; 4:1).

From this brief but rich introduction to The Principle of Sexuality, found in the book of Genesis, we move on to the New Testament teaching of mutuality in sexual matters within marriage. The key to understanding what the apostle Paul says about sex and sundry other things is the mutuality specified in the book of Ephesians: "Submit to one another out of reverence for Christ" (Ephesians 5:21, NIV).

With this basic guideline for all the relationships within Christian marriage in mind, ponder J. B. Phillips' translation of I Corinthians 7:3-5. "The husband should give his wife what is due to her as his wife, and the wife should be as fair to her husband. The wife has no longer full rights over her own person, but shares them with her husband. In the same way the husband shares his personal rights with his wife. Do not cheat each other of normal sexual intercourse, unless of course you both decide to abstain temporarily to make special opportunity for fasting and prayer. But afterwards you should resume relations as before, or you will expose yourselves to the obvious temptation of the devil."

The "obvious temptation of the devil" is not limited to the loss of genital fidelity through adultery. Much more likely among Christians, I think, is the loss of spiritual fidelity expressed in an absence of emotional support revealed by the thoughtlessness and lethargy of one's mate. This spiritual loss allows Satan to establish a seedbed in which feelings of self-pity, hostility and bitterness can take root. Thus, he has a chance to begin undermining your sense of unity by depriving you and your mate of the security of knowing—as an absolute certainty—that you are one. Our subject, therefore, is not frivolous but profoundly serious: The Principle of Sexuality.

There are two extreme, equally abnormal and potentially dangerous attitudes toward sex. One is epitomized by the person who talks about sex too much. The other is personified by the person who refuses to talk about sex at all.

The first might be termed the attitude of the pagan. We don't have to look long nor far for the cause of this particular phenomenon. According to Pitirim A. Sorokin, world famous sociologist, "A consuming interest in sex has so penetrated our national culture that it's been estimated we encounter some kind of sexual lure every nine minutes of our waking day."[1] In newspapers, books and magazines. On radio and television. From billboards and motion picture screens. In every conceivable way and through every possible medium, we are confronted with sex as the human body is flaunted before us in varying degrees of undress appealing to the base, the sensual and the crude. As a result of this malicious exploitation, our nation is reaping a whirlwind of tragic behavior, for we are a people beset by a hoard of pagans who talk about sex too much.

But just as dangerous, abnormal and extreme is the prude who refuses to talk about sex at all. The one who seems to believe that, if you ignore it, sex will go away.

The biblical Principle of Sexuality rejects both extremes. It refuses the philosophy of the pagan. It spurns the attitudes of the prude. Instead, it recognizes this powerful, natural force as something which was created by God and is therefore good in and of itself.

In Genesis 1:31 we are told that when God concluded His creative work "[He] saw everything that He had made, and behold, it was very good." Included in God's creative accomplishments was the human body with all of its complex capacities, hungers and drives. God called these good. So, if there's anything evil or smutty about sex and the human body, it's because we have made it so. In the beginning sex and the body were beautiful, pure and good.

And biblical Christianity has always said so. I know there are some muddle-headed prigs operating under the guise of Christians who have said sex is evil, that the body and pleasure are bad in themselves. But they're wrong. As C. S. Lewis points out, "Christianity is almost the only one of the great religions which thoroughly approves of the body—which believes that matter is good, that God Himself once took on a human body, that some kind of body is going to be given to us even in heaven and is going to be an essential part of our happiness, our beauty, and our energy...If anyone says that sex, in itself, is bad, Christianity contradicts him at once."[2]

Genesis 2:25 makes another profound statement regarding The Principle of Sexuality: "And the man and his wife were both naked and were not ashamed." Before the fall—before sin turned sex into the kinky thing it is for so many people today—Adam and Eve accepted their sexuality as a natural, beautiful thing about which they felt no cause to be ashamed.

They sensed instinctively what the Bible states clearly:

The sexual nature of mankind is a deliberate part of God's plan! *The good Lord didn't goof when He made the human body. It's of utmost importance that you and your mate understand this. In fact, marriage as God meant it to be will involve you in a joyous, easy, innovative, marriage-long sexual adventure with your mate.*

As two born-again Christians desiring God's best for your life, it is possible for you to enter the garden again, so to speak, and experience perfect marriage and—it's wonderful. This won't happen, however, unless—along with all the other principles under discussion—you understand intellectually and accept emotionally the biblical teaching regarding The Principle of Sexuality.

Sex and Marriage

The reason your sexuality is so significant is because, as George Sweazey points out, it combines two basic urges. Your urge for life and your urge for love. In sex, your life force and your love force are joined.[3] Sex, therefore, has to do with the very essence of your existence, psychologically as well as physically. Because sex is not just a physical hunger to be satisfied, but also represents a part of your person which is deeply spiritual, it is imperative for you and your mate to remember that, from the very beginning, it's by God's plan that one man and one woman should be joined together in one flesh through holy matrimony as the basic unit upon which the rest of society is built.

Various people have tried to improve on God's plan. In every age, in every land, under every conceivable condition, people have experimented with different ways of fulfilling the sex urge. But, they have always returned to that which God ordained from the beginning: one man and one woman, living together in the bonds of holy matrimony, as the one true way in which the deepest longings and desires of the human heart can be fulfilled.

If you go back into history, you'll discover that polygamy failed—not because somebody said it was wrong and started a crusade against it—but because it didn't satisfy the deepest needs of people. Even when the Bible records the polygamous nature of many homes in the Old Testament times, it is careful to point out the favoritism that persisted in those homes. The man almost always had one wife whom he loved above the others. She was his favorite. Not because he was perverse, but because he was normal. For the natural expression of human nature which cries out for fulfillment is one man and one woman becoming one flesh.

This perfect blending of two personalities cannot be achieved in a casual liaison, a transient passion or a clandestine affair. Sex outside of marriage is like tennis with the net down. It is devoid of the commitment to certain rules and boundaries which make it meaningful.

Therefore, one of the first things you and your mate must fully understand is that The Principle of Sexuality involves a commitment to marriage and to the home. In this setting sex is not only sanctioned, it is blessed by society and God. It is not only allowed, it is encouraged. For here, within the confines of marriage, one man and one woman, bound together by God in one flesh, are given the power and privilege of fulfilling the divine purposes for which sex was created.

The Mutuality of Sex

Before we get into some of the things God had in mind when He established The Principle of Sexuality, let me say that all sex within marriage is not good. As David W. Augsburger explains, "Both rape and prostitution can occur in marriage. The man who threatens or even abuses his wife to force sexual intercourse is committing rape. The woman who uses sex to manipulate her husband is committing prostitution."[4] Instead of money, her price may be acquiescence on his part to her will in various areas of their relationship. The biblical Principle of Sexuality is only fulfilled when sex in marriage is mutually willed and mutually controlled.

This is the point Paul is making in the passage from I Corinthians 7. He is saying that to function at its best, The Principle of Sexuality requires a commitment by you and your mate to the concept of mutuality as loving openness, vulnerability, caring and support. You are neither to deny or demand from each other, but voluntarily give to each other. The concept of marriage rights must be replaced by an understanding of marriage responsibilities— duties dictated by love, not law.

David R. Mace, the dean of Christian counselors, explains, "One of these [responsibilities] is the duty not to condemn your marriage partner to suffer a state of unrelieved sexual frustration. If you do this, you are asking for sustained love and loyalty while you are withholding the experience of unity in which love and loyalty of married couples is continually regenerated. That is unfair. Paul put it in stronger terms. He said that you are practicing a fraud (I Corinthians 7:5, KJV). You are not in fact giving, as part of the marriage contract, what in the eyes of the world you have undertaken to give to your wife or husband."[5]

It is not my purpose to stir up a lot of sub-Christian guilt about your not being the always willing, always available sex partner your marriage mate seems to need. There are any number of valid reasons why you may need to say no to your spouse at a particular time. But, if the two of you have previously established a loving relationship based upon a commitment to The Principle of Prevailing Atmosphere, your husband or wife won't have any trouble accepting a no which is rooted in self-giving love. It's when no is said in an unloving way you're in trouble.

Ann Landers spoke in our city some time back and commented on the familiar saying, "An apple a day keeps the doctor away." She added, "From the mail I receive, I've been led to conclude: 'A fight at night keeps the obstetrician in flight.' " She went on to say, "More divorces are caused by falling asleep than any other single act."

It has been my experience that most folks who are insensitive to the sexual advances of their mate act more out of ignorance than any other cause. They just don't understand how closely the love force and life force in their spouse are linked to his or her sense of sexuality and significance. Nor do they grasp the depths of devastation which occur when, through thoughtlessness or lethargy on their part, this keenly spiritual as well as physical part of their mate's needs is not met in the one place on this planet where they might expect it would be met—their own home.

David Mace speaks with profound accuracy when he says, "Married couples who call themselves Christians owe it to one another to take their sex relationship seriously; to give themselves to it wholeheartedly, striving to invest it with all the warmth and richness which it should have, for it is the God-given and sacramental expression of their mutual love."[6]

If you and your mate are having difficulty adjusting in this area, you need to know that in all probability the sexual problem is secondary rather than primary. Sex is like a barometer. It merely reflects the atmosphere around it, but does nothing to control the atmosphere. Sex is almost never the basic difficulty between partners. Nor is the solution to a sexual maladjustment merely to try harder. Usually that only leads to more painful failures.

The answer lies in a healing. A healing so deep that it touches your mind, the way you think; your emotions, the way you feel; and your will, the way you respond. If you are having trouble applying The Principle of Sexuality in your marriage, I urge you to set aside your pride and allow the Spirit of God to go to work in this area of your life. I also suggest you seek the assistance of a competent Christian marriage counselor whose confidential guidance and committed prayers can be of great help to you and your mate.

Sex and Creation

Let's look at some of the goals God had in mind when He established The Principle of Sexuality. The first purpose of sex in marriage is the creation of life. Genesis 4:1 explains that Adam knew Eve, his wife. She conceived and bore Cain saying, "I have gotten a manchild with the help of the Lord." Truly, there are few things more gratifying and up-lifting than the knowledge that, through an act of love, you and your mate become partners with God in the creation of new life.

If you are a parent, I'm sure you can remember the wonder you felt when you first looked down upon a squirm-ing bit of humanity and realized this was bone of your bone and flesh of your flesh. Can you remember that hallowed moment when you looked down upon your offspring with a sense of awe and realized your love had been the instru-ment through which an immortal soul was brought into being?

It was necessary for you and your mate to each unclasp one hand in order to make room for the new member of your tiny circle. But it was worth it, wasn't it! For, along with that little one came new joys as the two of you learned what it means to be God's deputy creators in the bringing of new life into being.

"Sex is our link to the past and our link to the future, and no Christian should enter into it without a deep and lasting sense of the sheer wonder of ongoing life. After all, our years on this earth are few enough, a mere 'moment between sun and frost.' But we are also part of an endless chain of life, and we are responsible to God and men to see that the chain does not break at our link, nor life be wasted because of our indifference or selfishness or lack of faith. In the mystery of sex is hidden the mystery of new life, and only the most shallow soul can be careless before that mystery."[7]

To me, one of the most moving and meaningful parts of the marriage ceremony comes when, as presiding minister, I turn to the father of the bride and say, "Who gives this woman to be married to this man?" And her dad replies, "Her mother and I." Then he turns, leaves the wedding party and is seated with his wife. To me there is great symbolism there. Portrayed in that little drama is the passing of one generation from the stage of life—a generation which has had its day in the creative partnership with God, has raised its children, brought new hope into the world—which now steps aside so another, younger, stronger, more eager generation may add its link to the chain of life as it, too, becomes a partner with God in the act of creation.

Sex as Communication

An even more basic aspect of The Principle of Sexuality than creation is communication. In a healthy Christian marriage, sex is a vivid form of deeply profound and meaningful communication.

As we discovered in our discussion of The Principle of Fullness Before Overflow, when Adam was involved in a warm, openhearted loving relationship with God, he enjoyed a blessed state of self-realization. He was a whole person. The atmosphere in which he lived was completely satisfying from Adam's point of view. But God, who had made him and knew him from head to toe, saw needs in Adam which Adam did not recognize in himself.

"Then the Lord God said [not Adam], 'It is not good for the man to be alone; I will make him a helper suitable for him' " (Genesis 2:18). Marriage then, as God meant it to be, is that mysterious amalgamation in which two people

115

begin as units of wholeness, yet find a form of completion in each other which they did not experience in their single state. They become "one flesh."

This means The Principle of Sexuality is not primarily concerned with propagation, although that's certainly an important function. Its dominant meaning is that of communication. It's a way of saying something to your mate: "Now that we are one, you are not alone. You are a vital part of me. I am a vital part of you. Without you, there is something gone from me. And though it boggles my mind, without me there is something gone from you."

In a world becoming increasingly and grimly impersonal, sex in marriage is a way of affirming your mate. Of saying: "You matter. You are not just a digit. A social security number. A punch hole in a computer card. You are a person. A human being of sublime significance."

There are several billion people on planet earth. Out of that vast number, there is only one person to whom you can say: "You are the other half of me." That statement has no meaning between you and a dozen other people—or one other person, for that matter. You are not one with that person or group of persons. It is your mate with whom you are one in a togetherness so holy, pure, pleasing and glorifying to God, that He inspired the Apostle Paul to use the mysterious welding process of Christian marriage as an illustration of the union between Christ and His church (Ephesians 5:32).

Sex in marriage is not something to be shunned. Or feared. Or entered into as a chore. You are the only person on this earth with the right, and thus responsibility, to say to your spouse: "You are not alone. You are a vital part of me." Because sex is a powerful means of communication, it should play a profoundly important part in your Christian marriage. It mirrors the totality of your relationship and therefore should reflect a fascinating variety, for everything else going on in your marriage will have an effect upon it.

In a happy and healthy Christian marriage sex can be "sublime and comic and beautiful and ordinary and refreshing and tiresome. It [can be] a delightful game and a loving bliss and an annoying disappointment."[8] Therefore, as George Sweazey points out, you and your mate "need to be sensitive to each other's changing moods. If one [of you] feels boisterous and the other has just been reading Mrs. Browning's sonnets, [you'll] need to get in tune. [You] should feel free to bumble and to laugh at [yourselves] without the anxieties of a space engineer during countdown."[9]

Because sex in marriage is a gift of God—ordained and blessed by Him as a means of communication—you and your mate should receive it with thanksgiving and exercise it with joy. As I have emphasized repeatedly, you are the only person on this planet with the right, and thus responsibility, to say to your mate in this most vivid way: "Now that God has made us one, you are not alone. You are a vital part of me."

Sex as Celebration

Which brings us around to the third application of The Principle of Sexuality in marriage—celebration. To celebrate something is to be in a joyful, thankful mood. The word "celebration" has a festive, fun-filled air about it. And, at its best, sex in marriage is a celebration of joy. It's an expression of your spiritual unity which is delightful, natural and playful. With refreshing candor, the Bible declares: "And the man and his wife were both naked and were not ashamed" (Genesis 2:25).

I write with all the reverence and restraint I can muster, for I know we are treading on holy ground. However, the exploiters of sex have said so much about technique, they've turned a relationship which God intended to be relaxed and comfortable into a performance. It's almost as

117

if each act of intercourse demands a grade. This has made sex serious in a way that's sick. Many people have become worried performers. When that happens, spontaneity is lost. Sex becomes work instead of play. A *labor* of love instead of an expression of joyful exuberance.

It needs to be said in a Christian context, and not just read on the pages of *Playboy* magazine, so let's say it: Sex is fun!

It is a God-ordained, God-blessed means of letting out the child in you, of having fun without feeling guilty or battering the family budget. But if it's going to be that, you must become aware of your mate's needs and moods. Learning to respond to each other is more than a physiological matter. It involves the totality of your being. It requires that both of you master the art of being sensitive to the other.

Sensitivity and understanding are important at all ages and stages of marriage. For instance, I was talking with one of my friends about how our needs change as we change, and he said, "These kids think they know about love. They're out driving, he runs out of gas, they smooch a little and she says she loves him. Shucks, that isn't love. It's when they've been married for 25 years, they're sitting in the living room one night smooching, he runs out of gas and she says she loves him—brother, that's love!"

Every age and stage of marriage requires that you practice sensitivity and understanding. As someone has said, the marriage knot cuts off circulation. Your mate becomes the only person on this planet you can touch. You become the only person on this planet your mate can touch. That's very confining. One out of several billion. But within that confinement there should be perfect freedom. Freedom to explore. To play. To grow. To learn to live and love together.

In all probability, the norm for your marriage will not be a situation in which you are both "turned on" all the time, or even at the same time. That's why it's necessary to learn *agape* love rather than rest your marriage on the sinking sand of *eros* love. *Eros* is interested in what it can get. *Agape* is concerned with what it can give. *Eros* demands. *Agape* responds. It voluntarily reaches out to meet the needs of your beloved without necessarily feeling a need yourself.

Jesus said, "Love your enemies" (Matthew 5:44). That was a revolutionary thought. Everyone loves his friends. Nothing is easier than to love the lovable. And nothing is easier than to make love when both you and your partner feel like it. That won't earn you any Brownie points. But when you respond to the need of your mate, even though you don't feel like it, that *will* put a star in your crown, because that's *agape* love in action. The kind of love which has its own rewards.

It's a physiological fact that you just can't always feel *eros*. But you can always give *agape if you will to*.

Agape love is not an emotion. It's an attitude. Your attitude is the one thing over which you have personal control. If you *will* to be in the right attitude, you can find it in your power to meet the needs of your mate whether you feel like it or not. Remember: no one else on this earth has that privilege.

At its best, celebration is the culmination of communication. That's why the sexiest thing a husband can do is to really listen to his wife. That is, my Christian brother, by your actions, as well as your attitudes, convey to her the message: "Honey, I'm really *with* you when I'm with you."

Because celebration is the natural culmination of effective communication, the sexiest thing a wife can do is reinforce her husband. That is, my Christian sister, by both word and deed let him know that, in your eyes at least, *he's okay!*

Sex in the Bible is never sex. It is always knowledge. Again and again, as the Hebrew speaks of the marriage relationship we read, "He *knew* his wife." Need I remind you that such knowledge does not come overnight. Such perfection of mutual understanding does not happen in the few moments it takes to repeat the marriage vows. It requires years to build a true and lasting friendship.

So, too, you and your mate can expect it will take years to really know each other. But finally, through a gradual increasing of intimacy, there will come a time when, in a grand and glorious amalgamation of body and soul, you become that perfect unity which God ordained from the beginning and called one flesh.

8

The Principle of Communication

Somewhere I remember reading the story of an old man who had seven stalwart sons. One day he called these big, husky boys around him and they came, each flexing his muscles like a wrestler to show how strong he was. The old man sat in a chair and pointed to a bundle of sticks lying on his lap. The sticks had been tied together with string.

"I'd like to know which one of you is able to break the bundle of sticks," he said.

The youngest boy answered impulsively, "I can do it, Father." He took the bundle and with all his strength tried to break it, but couldn't.

A second son tried without success, and then a third. Finally, after the seventh and oldest boy had failed in his attempt, they all agreed it couldn't be done.

"I'm surprised at you," the old man said. "Let me have it and I'll show you how I can break it." He laid the bundle of sticks across his lap, pulled out a single stick, and with hardly any effort broke it in two. Then, one by one, he repeated the process.

"Anyone could do it that way," the boys protested.

"You're right," the father responded, "and I want you to remember this lesson. You cannot be broken as long as you stick together. But when you begin to separate one from the other, each of you is easily broken until our whole family will be broken up."

It's an old story, but it vividly applies to a contemporary concern. If Satan cannot tear up the Body of Christ in huge hunks, as he has sometimes done in the past, he'll do it bit by bit by destroying individual cells within the Body. Therefore, you and your mate should take care to guard your marriage, for Satan is making an all-out assault against Christian homes in an effort to neutralize the influence of God's people in these latter days.

From the turn of the century until now, the ratio of divorces to marriages in our country has increased from one in twelve to one in four. In some areas it's one in three. For teenage marriages, I'm told, it may be as high as nine out of ten. Many of these broken marriages involve Christians.

But the ominous aftershock of this statistical bombshell is that these figures don't really tell the whole story. Many broken marriages never show up in the statistician's column, but the people involved are as totally divorced from each other as if they had gone to court. They live under the same roof, eat at the same table, even sleep in the same bed, but they're married singles. They have a piece of paper which says they belong to each other, but it's a marriage in name only. In every way which really counts, they're single.

A divorcee stopped by for supportive counsel. "The pain of divorce is very great," she said, "and the loneliness is hard to endure. But," she added with great emotion and not a few tears, "it's nothing compared to the loneliness in a marriage in which there is no communication. At least now I know I'm alone. I know what the ground rules are. Before, it was living hell. Not because I was mistreated physically, for I wasn't. I was just ignored. There was no communication, and the feeling of loneliness was unbearable."

Obviously, that kind of marriage falls far short of what the Heavenly Father had in mind when He established this relationship for His children.

Marriage was God's idea. Among other things, He meant it to be an antidote to loneliness. "It is not good for the man to be alone," God said. "I will make him a helper suitable for him" (Genesis 2:18). As we read on, in verses 19 and 20, we discover none of the creatures God brought to Adam met this need for companionship. "So the Lord God caused a deep sleep to fall upon the man, and he slept; then He took one of his ribs, and closed up the flesh in that place. And the Lord God fashioned into a woman the rib which He had taken from the man, and brought her to the man. And the man said, 'This is now bone of my bones, and flesh of my flesh; she shall be called Woman, because she was taken out of Man.' For this cause a man shall leave his father and his mother, and shall cleave to his wife; and they shall become one flesh" (verses 21-24).

It was God's intention, you see, that marriage be a way of countering aloneness through communication. But something happened to God's loving plan for His children. Sin happened. Satan moved into that idyllic, supportive atmosphere, sowed the seeds of alienation and discord, tangled up the lines of communication and turned the very relationship God had created to alleviate loneliness into a means of producing it. Truly Satan is the great deceiver who, as Jesus said, comes to steal, to kill and to destroy (John 10:10).

Unfortunately, many of his dirty tricks are succeeding in Christian homes. That's why it's imperative for you and your mate to take extra special care in guarding your home. It's also important for you to understand the profound difference between marriage as God meant it to be and marriage as it is so often portrayed by the world, the flesh and the devil. There is a tremendous difference between an acceptable marriage in the eyes of the world, and the great marriage God wants yours to be.

Married Singles

Every day of your life you and your mate are being conditioned by cliches, caricatures, stereotypes and culturally imposed roles to live a single lifestyle within marriage. Satan's technique is so subtle, and his approach so clever, many Christians are not even aware they have become married singles. They share bed and board together, but beyond that they really aren't involved with each other.

What are some of the things Satan uses to lead a Christian couple into a married singles lifestyle? Read on and perhaps you'll recognize a few: Work, work, work. The morning or evening newspaper. Television. Reading. Sports. The kids. An excessive preoccupation with the accumulation of things. Recreation which does not include your mate. Hobbies which are singular in nature. Friends who actually serve no other purpose than to keep the two of you from having to seriously encounter each other. Community activities. And yes, I'm sorry to say, sometimes even so-called "religious" activities, such as going to meetings.

Obviously, there's a lot of good in many of these things. Work, social awareness, hobbies, sports, community activities and even a certain degree of solitariness are all important in their place. Read Ecclesiastes 3 and you'll find there's time for this and a time for that. But when work, reading, sports, TV, socializing and these other things cluster together into a configuration of demands upon your time and energy which outrank your coupleness, your paired interests illustrated by the overlapping areas of the two rings on the frontispiece; and when your priorities are such that they do not build your marriage but push you toward becoming married singles—they need to be reexamined. Satan is using good for evil. Piece by piece he is pulling down the home God wants to help you build.

If, for any of the reasons I've listed—or others—you and your mate have become, or are on the verge of becoming, married singles, I'm sure this isn't the way you meant it to be when you married. The two of you stood before the marriage altar with the highest of intentions and ideals. But you see, good marriages are never accidental. Good communication is an art which, like any other art, must be mastered through hard work, discipline, practice and commitment.

David Augsburger has this to say about the art of communication:

> Partners vary greatly in their need for privacy or their readiness for intimacy. Some persons are compulsively eager to share everything with their partners and then demand that they reciprocate. But such a decision must be mutual. Others fear transparency and seek to protect their privacy at all cost.
>
> The desire for an intimate understanding of each other's emotional capacities is the base of good communications in marriage. But such intimate communication is not a note tendered in marriage and thereafter payable upon demand.
>
> Intimacy of mind is a gift. Freely given. It is offered, not upon request, but in response to another's willingness to open his or her self in sharing. As we sense acceptance, understanding and forgiveness extended to us by another, we are free to give love and trust.
>
> Such a relationship cannot be forced. Nothing stymies communication like the persistent prying of a partner who insists on "breaking and entering" another's privacy; although general understanding may often best result from conflict which cleans up old "grudge" items and clears the air for a more honest love relationship.
>
> Openness with each other is a skill which must be learned. It is not a talent possessed by some at birth like a musical ear. It's an ability to be acquired in maturing. Maturing in communication, maturing in handling conflict, maturing in giving and receiving love.[1]

A growing love relationship of intimacy is not easily achieved. It requires, as I have already said, hard work, commitment and continued practice.

Lucille and I never intended to become married singles. But, as we were sharing one morning—reflecting back upon the early years of our life together—she reminded me how she had been conditioned, as a little girl, to believe that a good wife and mother was one whose house was always spic-and-span, whose cooking was a gourmet's delight, and whose children were squeaky clean. So she worked night and day to make sure she measured up to that image. And she did.

"But don't you remember," she asked, "how many times you used to say, 'Honey, why don't you stop working? Why don't you just come and sit by me for awhile so we can be together?' "

Frankly, I didn't remember saying those things to her, because in that moment I was recalling how, as the demands of my career began to grow and my determination to be a good minister increased, I, too, had pushed us closer and closer to becoming married singles. Apart from my annual vacation, I never took a day off. Never. Seven days a week, ten to twelve hours a day, month after month after month, was standard operating procedure. Once in a while, perhaps every other year, we'd manage a two or three day break. Usually both of us were so uptight, so unaccustomed to a time of relaxation, we didn't know what to do with it and failed to make the most of it.

During those years, I rarely had a night at home. In fact, one of my ministerial buddies and I were reminiscing about the time we sat together in a Chicago coffee shop comparing date books. He had served a sister church in the Windy City during part of the time I ministered there. His records showed he hadn't been at home in the evening for 42 nights in a row. With perverse pride, I took great delight in pointing out I had beaten him by two. I had worked 44 nights straight.

The tragedy is that both of us thought we were being virtuous. We honestly believed that by responding to the needs of other families at the expense of our own we were serving Jesus. In reality, we were being suckered by Satan into creating conditions at home which were perilously close to a married singles lifestyle.

You can imagine how shocked I was, therefore—after working ten to twelve hours a day, seven days a week for years—when one day Lucille, in a moment of loving candor, asked me, "John, do you know what my primary image of you is?"

If I had thought about it for a thousand years, I never would have come up with the right answer. For when I told her "no," she said, "My primary image of you is lying flat on your back."

That really pushed my hostility button. Believe me, I was angry. Here I was, breaking my neck for Jesus, and she had an image of me lying flat on my back!

When I cooled down (about five days later), I began to think seriously about what she was trying to say to me. I asked the Holy Spirit to give me understanding, because obviously, what she had said was a desperate effort to communicate something to me. As I thought about it—as I put myself inside her skin, as it were—it suddenly dawned on me she was exactly right.

Lucille has always been an early riser. When the children were small (except for Sundays when I got up at 5:00 a.m. to prepare myself spiritually for my preaching responsibility that day), she was often up first. What did she see? Right! J.A.L. flat on his back.

After a long day of responding to the needs of people I would come home for supper exhausted. Instead of being the loving initiator of companionship through conversation about her and her needs, I grabbed the evening paper to lie down for a few minutes before dinner. Or, sometimes I'd lie down to watch the evening news on TV. What was her image of me? Flat on my back.

After a hasty supper during which I made little effort to communicate—because after all, I had been communicating with people all day—I'd stretch out for a few minutes more. Then I'd hoist myself up, give her and the kids a peck on the cheek, jump in the car and begin my evening work. Usually it was quite late by the time I got home and I'd flop into bed. Lucille, if she was still awake, got as her last view at night the same one she had gotten in the morning: John Allan Lavender, flat on his back!

After I got over the anger, frustration and whopping chunk of self-pity generated by her loving candor, I began to think about what I could do to change her image of me. Even more important, I was anxious to do something about the married singles lifestyle I was contributing to as a workaholic.

I reasoned that Lucille would probably always be a morning person and I would probably always be a night person. I hadn't yet rearranged my priorities (that was to come almost ten years later), so my job still came ahead of everything else. Sometimes, I'm ashamed to say, even ahead of my relationship to Jesus. Therefore, at that time, I couldn't see how I could do much about the structure of my workday except for the brief period around dinner time.

So I made a conscious, deliberate decision. I decided to remind myself each evening that my day didn't end when I drove in the driveway. I still had responsibilities, but they were obligations spawned by love for the people I care about most—my wife and children. I decided to become a loving initiator of creative communication.

While I haven't always succeeded (there have been many times when I slipped back into the old mold), I usually go into the kitchen, give Lucille a hug and ask if there is something I can do to help. Peel the carrots, maybe, or set the table. If supper is ready we just chat about the day. On occasion Lucille will observe that I'm very tired and say, "Why don't you go and lie down for a little while?" But now it's her idea.

Often I help clean up the dishes after dinner. And then we can sit down together and make a conscious effort to reach out to each other for the closeness we both need to offset the pressures Satan would use to pull us apart.

One evening, during a beautiful time of sharing, Lucille communicated to me a growing sense of *being* married. Not just that we *were* married on September 1, 1946, but that we are *being* married today. Right now. This very minute. That we are involved in something which is still in the making. Something which is in the process of becoming. Something alive and active. We are *being* married.

As she shared that beautiful, electrifying thought with me, and we tried to describe to each other how we felt about *being* married—about being caught up in a living, growing relationship—we were enveloped by the very love of God. We sensed, in that moment, what our Heavenly Father had been talking about when He said, "And they shall *become* one flesh."

Lucille and I are not the same people we were on September 1, 1946. We're not the same people we were a year, a month, or even a week ago. Nor are we the people we're going to be. Even as we are *being* married, we are *being* saved (Acts 2:47).

That is to say, our God who is alive is alive in us! He is taking the various parts of our human nature, bringing them bit by bit into submission to His Holy Spirit, and, as a result, we are *being* saved. We are *being* converted bit by bit, day by day. As this happens to us individually, it has a profound effect upon us corporately. Our coupleness is strengthened. We discover a little bit more of what it means to be one flesh.

Now, if that can happen to a couple of veterans like us with so many things militating against us, it can happen in your marriage. Maybe you and your spouse are like the husband and wife who told me their idea of spending an evening together was watching TV. In different rooms!

"We thought we were involved with each other," they said, "but now we see how very uninvolved we really were."

Every marriage goes through three stages. There's the honeymoon stage which is characterized by a kind of giddy, almost heady delight. Then there's the humdrum stage, which is marked by a grim, sometimes hurtful disillusionment. It's a time when openness is often shut off because you are too threatened to be honest and vulnerable.

If your marriage happens to be in this middle stage right now, you may find the virtues of your mate actually irritate you. The very things you once admired and were attracted to now bug you. Petty annoyances become huge stumbling blocks. And somewhere back in your subconscious mind is the terrifying thought that *your* marriage—the marriage that was going to be perfect—is just like all the rest. Well, there's hope! Beyond the honeymoon stage and the humdrum stage, there is the healthy stage. It represents God's ideal for you and is characterized by grace and growing joy.

No marriage, even a great one, is constantly in stage three. The cycles recur. Marriage is not a static experience any more than the Spirit-filled life is a static state. If you don't faithfully practice The Principle of Fullness Before Overflow, you will find yourself slipping back into stage two. It may occur monthly. Weekly. Daily. Even hourly. But there's something you and your mate can do about it.

You can decide to love. Daily. Momentarily. Repeatedly. For love is not a feeling, love is a decision!

When you say, "I can't love my mate anymore," you're really saying, "I won't love him or her anymore." Love is not something you feel. It is something you do. Something you decide. And because God gave you free will, love is a decision you and your mate have the power to make—daily.

There are two quotations which have taken on profound meaning for Lucille and me. First, "Love is a daily decision."[2] It is something each of us can *will* to do. Daily.

130

Hourly. The true life of love is not lived in the emotions. It is lived in the will. We can *will* to love and be loved, even though there are times we may feel unloving or unlovable. Out of all the people on this planet, Lucille, alone, is the other half of me. I, alone, am the other half of her. Therefore, we have it within our power to decide to be with and for each other.

As someone has said, "A happy marriage requires that you fall in love many times, always with the same person." I don't happen to think you *fall* into love. Love is something you *climb* into. But, however you say it, the truth remains: "Love is a daily decision."

The second quotation which is growing in its power and meaning to us is the simple phrase, "Happiness is a habit."[3] God has given us the freedom and capacity to experience His joy and share that joy with each other. Like everyone else on planet earth, we, too, are creatures of habit. Over the decades of our relationship together, Lucille and I have made some bad habits. But, by God's amazing grace, we're learning to break those bad habits and replace them with good ones. The habit of happiness. The habit of hope. The habit of healing. We're doing it through a daily decision to give loving acceptance and forgiveness to each other.

Hindrances to Good Communication

I heard about a couple who were allowing their hobbies to push them perilously close to becoming married singles. He liked to read. She liked to knit. One night, in an effort to build a bridge of communication, she said, "Honey, why don't you read to me while I knit?" With incredible insensitivity, he replied, "I've got a better idea. You knit to me while I read!"

Two hindrances to good communication which must be overcome are the bad habits of lazy listening and hasty speaking. The confusion which results can be more tragic than comic.

A disgruntled customer of a do-it-yourself catalog firm sent a letter of complaint to the company: "I built a birdhouse according to your stupid plans. Not only is it too big, but it keeps blowing out of the tree. Signed, Unhappy." The reply came back, "Dear Unhappy: Sorry. We accidentally sent you a sailboat blueprint. If you think you are unhappy, you should see the guy who came in last at the Yacht Club Regatta in a leaky birdhouse."

As we've learned, there are no stereotypes which stand up under examination. So there's probably no better advice for both men and women than that which is given in James 1:19: "Let everyone be quick to hear, [and] slow to speak." Again, that takes discipline and time, because good communications are not established overnight.

A middle-aged man was beginning to lose his hair. Finally, he had one hair left on his head. He faithfully oiled and massaged that single strand until one morning he got out of bed and there on the pillow lay that one last hair. In great anguish he cried out, "Great Scott, I'm bald!"

Just as a man with one hair doesn't grow bald overnight, so too—if you've allowed the lines of communication to get tangled—you and your mate will not unsnarl them on the first try. You must keep on keeping on. Effective application of The Principle of Communication takes sustained commitment and tenacity. To communicate well means mastering the art of being "quick to hear and slow to speak."

The Revolving Discussion Sequence

A little game that can help you do this is called RDS, or the Revolving Discussion Sequence. It's a communications game designed to help you and your mate arrive at a compromise in which no one wins at the expense of the other's losing. The rules of the game are simple.

One of you makes a statement. Before the other person can reply, he or she must restate, to the first person's satisfaction, what the first person said. When you have established a clear understanding that what the first person said is what the second person heard, the second person must find a way to agree with that. If there is total agreement, you don't have a problem. However, you may not agree entirely with what your mate said, so you reply in a manner such as this: "I can agree there's considerable truth in what you say." Or you may grudgingly admit, "There's a grain of truth there." If you don't agree at all, you simply agree that this is how your mate thinks and affirm his or her right to that opinion.

After the statement, restatement and agreement, the second person is free to make his or her statement. Again, before the mate can reply, he or she must restate, to the satisfaction of the second person, what that person said and find a way to agree with it. This process is continued until the matter is resolved.

So the rules are simple: statement, restatement and agreement...statement, restatement and agreement. Hence the name: Revolving Discussion Sequence. The goal of the game, as I've said, is a compromise in which nobody wins at the expense of the other person's losing.

Let me show you how it works. A young couple came in for premarital counseling and, in the process of our conference, we spent time practicing RDS. The rules are simple, but it's hard to play because it requires breaking the bad habits of lazy listening and hasty speaking.

I asked them if there was an area of controversy or misunderstanding they were trying to work through. They both grinned and said, "Yes, a car." It turned out they needed a new car. Both agreed it should be a compact car. However, she wanted a VW and he wanted a Toyota. We decided they would play this little game to see if they could arrive at a solution.

"You go first," he said.

She replied by saying, "I think we ought to get a Volkswagen."

He restated this accurately and agreed that was her opinion and she had a right to it. (Which meant that he didn't agree at all!) Then he made his statement. "I think we ought to get a Toyota."

She dutifully restated this to him accurately and agreed that was his opinion and he had a right to it. (Which, likewise, meant she didn't agree at all!)

So after two levels we had managed to establish the fact they didn't agree.

She went on to say, "I think we ought to get a VW because they're very popular. Every time you turn around you see one on the street."

He responded by saying, "You feel we ought to get a Volkswagen because they are popular." She nodded, and he agreed that was probably true. "But," he said, "I think we ought to get a Toyota because they are easier to work on, they don't require a special set of tools," and he went through a whole series of logical reasons as to why he thought a Toyota was the superior automobile.

She listened faithfully, carefully restated what he had said, to his satisfaction, and agreed everything he had said was probably true and made a lot of sense. "But," she said, "the other day I was over at my girl friend's house. She has a VW and I was sitting in it. She said, 'Oh, Cindy (not her real name), you look so cute in that car. I can just imagine how you'll look tooling around town in one just like it.' "

Her young fiance was a very smart fellow. With a great big grin, he said, "Boy, I can certainly agree with that! You'd look great driving around town in any car. In fact, honey, you'd look great on a bicycle built for two!" I could tell by the smile she gave him that he'd earned himself some Brownie points with that response!

Then he sobered and said, "Honey, it's because you are

so pretty that I don't want you to have a VW." He explained how a number of years ago, in a much earlier model, a friend of his had been in an accident. The gas tank, which is in the front of the car, exploded and his buddy burned to death. "I'm sure they've corrected that hazard," he said, "but, honey, with that awful memory in my mind I could never be at ease with the thought of you driving that particular make of automobile."

She was quiet for a moment, then said, "Do you mean the reason you don't want me to have a VW is because you're afraid for my safety?"

"That's right," he nodded.

She thought a bit and then said, "Do you think we could find a cute Toyota?"

Now both those kids had a form of power, and both of them could have exercised their power to win. He could have said, "Look, I pay the bills. We're going to buy a Toyota whether you like it or not." And he would have won. But in the process he would have lost, because every time something went wrong with the car he would never hear the end of it. "That dumb Toyota won't start again this morning." "That dumb Toyota stalled in the street." "That dumb Toyota has got a flat tire."

On the other hand, she had a form of power and could have used it to win. She could have manipulated him into buying the car she wanted. But having won she would have lost, because every time something went wrong with it, he would have said, "You wanted it, you fix it!"

As it was, by employing the game of RDS, they avoided the dual pitfalls of lazy listening and hasty speaking. They made an honest effort to understand each other and to find a basis for agreement. When they finally got on the feeling level where she could get inside his skin and understand he wasn't being obstreperous or difficult, but was trying to cope with feelings he didn't fully grasp himself, they were able to arrive at a compromise in which nobody won at the expense of the other person's losing.

Several weeks later, after the wedding, she turned up in church. As she was going out the door she said, "Hey, Preacher, we got a Toyota. Plaid top. Special interior. The works. I look great in it!"

This little game can also work between parents and children. Parents have a form of power and so do youngsters. Each of them can use that power in a way designed to win. But whenever they win through an exercise of power alone, they lose. Something goes out of the trust relationship between them. However, through the simple process of statement, restatement and agreement, many problems can be avoided or solved. Whenever you have two people trying to understand each other, who find a way of agreeing with each other, you have two people who have taken a giant step toward that blessed experience of unity which scripture calls one flesh.

Actually, when you stop to think about it, scripture is full of appeals to the children of God to practice The Principle of Communication. "Let your speech always be with grace, seasoned, as it were, with salt, so that you may know how you should respond to each person" (Colossians 4:6). "For let him who means to love life and see good days refrain his tongue from evil and his lips from speaking guile" (I Peter 3:10). "A man has joy in an apt answer, and how delightful is a timely word!" (Proverbs 15:23). "He who gives an answer before he hears, it is folly and shame to him" (Proverbs 18:13). "Do you see a man who is hasty in his words? There is more hope for a fool than for him" (Proverbs 29:20). And in Proverbs 25:11 a proper application of The Principle of Communication is described this way: "A word fitly spoken is like apples of gold in pictures of silver" (KJV).

Romans 15:5-7 is not specifically addressed to marriage partners, but it certainly indicates the kind of communication model which ought to be practiced by all true lovers: "Now may the God who gives perseverance and encouragement grant you to be of the same mind with one another according to Christ Jesus: that with one accord you may with one voice glorify the God and Father of our Lord Jesus Christ. Wherefore, accept one another, just as Christ also accepted us to the glory of God."

Why does the Bible have so much to say about The Principle of Communication? Because, as Paul explains in Ephesians, it's God's intention that the world shall be able to look at your Christian marriage and see a direct correlation between it and the Body of Christ (Ephesians 5:32). Your Christian home is to be a microcosm of the church. A fellowship of love which is so special—a comradeship so close—people can look at it and say, "That's the church in miniature. That's a living example of what being a Christian is all about."

One evening a young husband arrived home and his wife said, "A strange thing happened today. The new minister at the church on the corner where we go occasionally stopped to ask me a question."

"What did he ask?" her husband inquired.

"He wanted to know if Jesus lives here."

"What did you say?"

"Well, I didn't know what to say."

"Didn't you tell him we are respectable people?"

"He didn't ask that."

"Didn't you tell him we go to church occasionally?"

"He didn't ask that, either."

"Didn't you tell him we read the Bible sometimes?"

"But he didn't ask that. *He asked if Jesus lives here.*"

God grant that you and your mate will translate the simplicity of that question into some of the involved complexities of your everyday life. By practicing The Principle of Communication, may you succeed in creating an atmosphere which will let everyone know Jesus lives in your home and is comfortable there. And as His Spirit is expressed in the way you speak to each other, you will be making it known that Jesus is indeed the silent participant in every conversation.

9

The Principle of Submission as Strategy

Our assumption thus far has been that you and your mate are Christians and are both earnestly seeking God's best for your marriage.

In this chapter, because Scripture requires it, there is a decided shift in emphasis. Our concern at this point turns to God's guidance to Christians who have non-Christian mates. This does not mean, however, that because you are blessed with a Christian spouse, you can afford to gloss over this section. The Principle of Submission as Strategy applies equally well to the problems involved in responding creatively to a Christain mate who may be in a carnal state from time to time.

The Spirit-filled life is not a static thing. It requires constant refills in order to stay full. Since all God's children are subject to Satan's oppression daily, there is the real likelihood that, even though you and your mate are Christians, problems rooted in carnality will arise from time to time. So the principle spelled out in I Peter—The Principle of Submission as Strategy—has wide application, and I ask you to give God every possible opportunity to instruct you through His written Word.

The New Testament references which have guided us thus far all assume, in fact require, that both you and your mate are Christians. They spell out, as I have said, the biblical principles for *Christian* marriage. When we come to I Peter, we have an entirely different situation on our hands. The counsel given here presupposes that your mate

138

is not a Christian and that your motivation is that he or she may be won to the Lord.

The premise Peter puts forward is quite simple: if the great commission is true, and you, as a Christian, are called to the task of world evangelism, then in your little world—the world of your community, your job and your home—submission is the best way to carry out your task.

Let's see how Peter develops this thesis. The first thing you need to note is that it's difficult, if not impossible, to divide up the book of I Peter, for this lovely little letter really is a single piece of correspondence with a single theme. To Christians who are under severe persecution and whose faith is being sorely tested, the Apostle says, "Keep cool under fire. Jesus, whose name you bear, will see you through. Do as He did when He was under attack. Resist the devil. You are in God's hands."

Submission as Witness in Your Community

Peter applies these words of exhortation to a variety of situations. In chapter 2, verse 13, he says, "Submit yourselves for the Lord's sake [that is, the sake of your Christian witness] to every human institution." In verse 11, he identifies their challenge to be "aliens and strangers," or as J. B. Phillips puts it, "strangers and temporary residents in this world." In verse 12, he tells them to maintain good conduct so that their total lifestyle causes their current critics to ultimately glorify the Lord for what they see in them. Then, in verse 13, he applies The Principle of Submission as Strategy to every human institution, making special reference in the following verses to civil authority, so that "by doing right you may silence the ignorance of foolish men" (verse 15).

Let me set the scene for you. It was 2,000 years ago.

139

Because of the radical, life-changing power of Jesus, Christians (at least those who were taking Him seriously), were being called people who turned the world upside down (Acts 17:6). They earned this reputation, not because they were anarchists or troublemakers in the traditional sense, but because, as their priorities and values began to change, it wasn't always good for business. Acts 16:16-24 records an interesting illustration of this.

To silence the people who were slandering the followers of Christ by spreading false rumors about them, Peter counsels: Bend over backwards to be good citizens and good neighbors so your sweet spirit of submission will speak for itself."

Submission as Witness on Your Job

His second application of this principle is more specific. "Servants, be submissive to your masters with all respect, not only to those who are good and gentle, but also to those who are unreasonable" (I Peter 2:18). William Barclay estimates there were about 60,000,000 slaves in the Roman Empire.[1] In the eyes of Roman law, a slave was not a person. He or she was a thing. It's easy to understand, therefore, why the common people—most of whom were servants and slaves—listened to Jesus gladly (Mark 12:37). He gave them dignity and hope. He pointed them to their higher humanity. By the time Peter got around to writing his first letter, the vast majority of Christians came from the servant class.

The essence of what Peter says to these people (I Peter 2:18-25) is as follows: Your best witness for Christ is being a good worker on your job. In fact, be better than the best. Even if your boss is a scoundrel, serve him faithfully, for that's what Christ would do. Jesus didn't come to be served. He came to serve, and suffered in the process. This is your mission, too. "For you have been called for this purpose, since Christ also suffered for you, leaving you an example for you to follow in His steps" (verse 21).

Submission as Witness in Your Home

When we move on to chapter 3, Peter applies The Principle of Submission as Strategy to marriages in which the mates are not equally yoked together spiritually. The wife is married to a non-Christian husband. Or the husband is married to a non-Christian wife.

It may seem strange that Peter's advice to women is six times longer than his counsel to men. He devotes the first six verses of chapter 3 to women and only verse 7 to men. However, this is probably true for at least two reasons.

First off, undoubtedly, women outnumbered men in the early church, even as they do today. Women have always been drawn to the Savior, because Jesus really was the best friend women ever had. We haven't space to go into all the contributions Christ made to the liberation of women, but the fact is that since His coming, the world of women has never been the same. We still have a long way to go—some of us are just now beginning to grasp the true significance of what He said and did—but right from the beginning it was clear to the women who listened to what Jesus was saying and observed the way He related to them as persons, that here was Somebody—with a capital "S"— a Very Special Person to whom they were attracted in great numbers.

A second reason for Peter's lengthy and detailed counsel to Christian wives as contrasted to his more brief instruction to Christian husbands is that, in the world Peter knew, a woman had no rights at all. Whether she lived under Jewish, Greek or Roman law, she was essentially a thing owned by her husband in the same way he owned any other possession. Therefore, if a husband became a Christian and, in his spiritual infancy, wanted to manipulate his wife, he could do so. From all outward appearances at least, she would become a Christian because her husband told her to.

On the other hand, if a wife were to become a Christian while her husband didn't (and that obviously happened in thousands upon thousands of first-century homes), she created an acute problem for herself.[2] She had no legal leverage to use on him, yet her conversion put her in jeopardy if her pagan husband decided he didn't want a *Christian thing* around the house.

Aware of this serious sociological problem, as well as the possibility that spiritually immature men might try to manipulate their wives into becoming Christians, Peter offers some advice which is not only profoundly simple, but simply profound. Here it is: *The best way to win those you care about the most is through the silent preaching of a Spirit-filled life.*

Remember, the premise throughout this entire section for citizens, common laborers and married Christians is the same: If the great commission is true, and you, as a Christian, are called to the task of world evangelism, then in your little world—the world of your community, your job and your home—submission is the best way to carry out your task.

Obviously, that won't be easy. When Fritz Kreisler, the great violinist, was at the apex of his career, he was approached backstage one night by an enthusiastic fan who said, "Oh, Mr. Kreisler, I'd give my life to play as you do."

"Madame," he replied quietly, "I did."[3]

Well, as I'm sure you've discovered, in marriage as in music, greatness is not achieved without serious commitment and hard work. And if your marriage is one in which your mate is not a Christian, or if he or she is a Christian but is not living a Spirit-filled life, then to lead your beloved into an experience of God's best may require that you give your life to that purpose. But wouldn't it be worth it if, as a result of your submission, he or she were to experience God's best? Of course it would!

Submission as Voluntary Selflessness

Before we go on to examine how The Principle of Submission as Strategy works as God's way of helping you win your mate, let's reveiw, very briefly, what it means to submit.

The word submission comes from the Greek word *hupotasso.* As we learned in chapter 4, *hupotasso* can be, and in some passages of scripture is, used as a military term to signify externally imposed subjection based on rank. However, when the verb is used in any of the marriage passages (Colossians 3, Ephesians 5, Titus 2, I Peter 3), *hupotasso* always appears, without exception, in the middle, or passive voice, which switches it from something that is done to you to something which you do to yourself voluntarily.

Therefore, the submission to which you as a Christian are called, is not something which is externally imposed on you by your mate. Instead, it is an internalized response to your mate which springs naturally and voluntarily from your heart because you are committed to following the example of Jesus who gave Himself freely and willingly in order that you might experience God's best.

In other words, a proper application of The Principle of Submission as Strategy is the antithesis of a jealous insistence on your rights, or a spirit of self-assertiveness. If the cross says anything, it is that God was ready to go to the limit to let you know He loves you and wants you to be reconciled to Him. There was nothing self-assertive or manipulative about Jesus. He never insisted on His rights, though He had every right to do so. Instead, "He humbled Himself by becoming obedient . . ." (Philippians 2:8).

Here, again, you find a form of the verb *hupotasso,* suggesting voluntary submission. As the New English Bible

143

has it, "He humbled *himself,* and in obedience, *accepted* even death. Death on a cross." (Italics are author's.) There is nothing assertive, pushy or manipulative about that, is there! And, yet, as the old gospel hymn declares, "Love so amazing, so divine, demands my soul, my life, my all."

It's impossible to get away from that kind of love. There's something about That Man on that cross and the fact He was there *willingly* because He loves me which gets to me. He doesn't try to manipulate me, but in the end He wins me through the overwhelming power of self-giving, self-humbling love.

So I repeat. *A proper application of The Principle of Submission as Strategy is the antithesis of a jealous insistence on your rights, or a spirit of self-assertiveness. It is not a manipulative process in which you are interested in winning over your mate. Rather, it is a redemptive process in which you are interested in winning your mate over to Christ.*

Beware of Satan's Subtle Deception

Satan is the great deceiver. He has a near-perfect counterfeit for all the real things the Spirit of God is trying to teach you. One of his tricks is to turn The Principle of Submission as Strategy into a form of manipulation so that, despite all outward appearances of submissiveness, on the inside—in the area of your attitudes—you're a rebel. If you allow Satan to succeed in twisting your motives, submission will not reflect a self-giving love full of concern for your mate, but a self-centered love which is more concerned for what the salvation of your mate will mean to you.

Louis H. Evans, Sr. tells of a woman who came to her minister complaining that she had prayed for her husband without success for seven years. "Prayer simply does not work!" she said.

Her pastor inquired, "Why do you want the salvation of your husband? Are you asking it for 'the glory of God'?"

"What do you mean, asking 'for the glory of God'?" she retorted. "Is not requesting the conversion of anyone asking 'for the glory of God'?"

Her minister replied, "Give me your reasons for desiring your husband's conversion, if you know them."

"Well," the wife said, "first of all I think that if he were a Christian he wouldn't be so mean to me. Our life would be more pleasant together."

"Selfish reason number one," her pastor replied. "Any other?"

"Well, yes; if he were a Christian he would go to church with me and save me the embarrassment, when I sit alone in the sanctuary, of the community's feeling that I was married to a pagan."

"Your embarrassment again. Selfish reason number two. Any other?"

"Yes, if he were a Christian I think we two could team up together and raise our children to better advantage. Then they would probably not stub their toes and we would not have to hang our heads in the community."

"So *you* would not have to hang *your* head. Selfish reason number three. Now, my dear lady, this is a purely selfish prayer. You should pray in this way and genuinely mean it: 'Dear Heavenly Father, I ask for my husband's conversion for Your glory, and Your glory alone. You love him. You want to save him and use him, and he needs You. Save him, I pray, for the sake of Jesus, in whose name I pray.' "

According to Dr. Evans, the woman went home and prayed that prayer earnestly and honestly. A week later she reported that her prayer had been answered.[4]

The key, in her case, was learning to recognize how Satan had perverted The Principle of Submission as Strategy by turning it into a very subtle form of manipulation which was designed to serve her own selfish desires. When she began to pray unselfishly—when she began to practice The Principle of Submission as Strategy in a self-giving way—the Spirit of God was free to work through her and her prayers to win her husband.

Some time ago *Eternity* magazine carried an article by a Christian layman with the lead line, "When I stopped praying for my wife and children great things happened."[5] That sentence was so intriguing I just had to read the rest of the article.

In it the author, John M. Drescher, tells how, for years, he had prayed for his wife and children but nothing much happened until it occurred to him he was praying incorrectly. He came to realize that, if his children were ever to know the love of Christ, he, as their father, needed to experience more of Christ's love himself, and make that love visible to them.

So he began to pray, "Lord, make *me* fit to live with, loving and kind like You are to me." He goes on to say, "I stopped praying solicitous prayers for my wife when I realized that my job was not to make her good, but to make her happy." He concludes by writing, "Something happened when I wanted God to change *me* more than I wanted Him to change the other persons."

As I read John Drescher's testimony, I said, "Praise God, that's it! That's The Principle of Submission as Strategy at its best! Wanting God to change me more than wanting Him to change the people around me."

Some weeks ago, I was talking to a lady in our town who, though seriously wanting to live a Spirit-filled life, had fallen prey to Satan's subtle deception in her attitudes at home. Instead of trying to love her husband through a period of carnality back into a Spirit-filled state, she had attempted to manipulate him and his moods in order to make him easier to live with.

"Things really began to improve," she told me, "when, after a very unpleasant scene at home, I was driving to work one day, and the Lord said, 'If I met you tonight and asked you how it was today between you and Dave, what would you say?'

"I answered, 'Why, Lord, You know what I'd have to say.'

"Immediately," she went on, "I knew where a change had to begin. To others I may have appeared to be a loving, supportive wife, but inwardly I was extremely rebellious. So I asked God to go to work on me. And He did." She paused, smiled and then added with joy, "John, you just wouldn't believe the change in my husband!" Again, The Principle of Submission as Strategy as it ought to be applied.

A professor took a mouse from the cage where it lived with other mice and put it in a special cage equipped with a bell operated by a tiny pedal on the floor. "Observe," he told his pupils, "every time I drop in a crumb of cheese, I tap the bell. Eventually the mouse will associate the bell with the cheese and ring it himself."

Sure enough, the mouse responded by jumping on the pedal, eating the cheese which was dropped to him and sitting down to wait for more. Put back in its regular cage after the experiment, the mouse was greeted by his friends and family.

"How did things go today?" his wife asked.

"Oh, fine," said the mouse. "A few more sessions and I'll have that human really conditioned. Every time I ring the bell, he drops in the cheese."

Sometimes it's hard to tell who's manipulating whom! In any case, manipulation was the last thing God had in mind when He inspired Peter to set forth this profound principle. And because there is a serious risk that The Principle of Submission as Strategy can be perverted by Satan into a form of manipulation, you must constantly be on guard against the adversary. If you let him, Big Red will deceive you into believing the outward appearance of submission is an adequate compensation for a rebellious spirit inside. It isn't! Therefore, a proper application of this prin-

147

ciple requires that you be on guard against the adversary's constant attempt to confuse you.

Lean Hard on the Holy Spirit

It also demands that you stay as close to the Lord as possible. If your mate is unsaved, or perhaps is a carnal Christian, it will take more than your human best to effectively practice The Principle of Submission as Strategy. *It will take your human best filled with the Holy Spirit.* Don't ever think you can pull it off alone. You can't. What you are being called to do is absolutely contrary to the flesh. It can only be accomplished in the fullness of the Spirit. But, praise God, you have His promise to give the Holy Spirit to those who ask Him (Luke 11:13). So ask. God will give you the grace you need to minister to your mate in a redemptive way. That's a promise!

What did the Holy Spirit have in mind when He inspired Peter to counsel Christians interested in winning a mate for the Lord to practice The Principle of Submission as Strategy? To begin with, as William Barclay points out, it might be well to take note of what Peter did not advise. For one thing, if you're a woman, he did not advise you to leave your husband. For another, he did not tell you to preach, to argue and to nag. Nor did he tell you to insist on your rightful freedom as a Christian. What, then, did he tell you? He told you something so simple you may find it hard to believe. He counsels you to be nothing more nor less than a good wife.[6]

A chap who wasn't in the habit of attending church began to show up quite regularly every Sunday morning. The pastor was delighted to see him and told him so. "It sure makes me feel good to see you in church with your wife."

"Well, Parson," the prodigal replied, "it's a matter of choice. I'd rather hear your sermon than hers." Obviously, that was *not* a wise application of the principle we're discussing. A heavy-handed approach might work in certain situations, but it won't work with most people, at least not for long. And it certainly could never, ever be called a proper application of The Principle of Submission as Strategy.

Do you know how a female rhinoceros selects her mate? William Coleman describes the process in an article which appeared in the *Moody Monthly* sometime back. He says, "She is nearsighted, so when she sees her beau, she first backs up. Then she charges him at thirty miles an hour, hitting him broadside and knocking him to the ground. Then she proceeds to gouge and step on him. When he is literally bleeding and bruised he gets the message, 'She loves me!' "[7]

Well, people are not rhinos, and no one, be they male or female, really appreciates a hard-nosed, heavy-handed, super-aggressive approach. Knowing this, the Holy Spirit inspired Peter to explain to you—as a Christian wife—that far more effective than any amount of preaching or nagging is what the Holy Spirit calls "the imperishable jewel of a gentle, quiet spirit" (see I Peter 3:3,4). When this is backed up by outward adornment which is tasteful and discreet (I Peter 3:3-7), it is well-nigh irresistible.

I was with a couple of church leaders one evening and mention was made of a Christian lady whom the three of us knew. "The neat thing about her," one person said, "is that she's as beautiful on the inside as she is on the outside, and she never, ever dresses in a way which draws so much attention to her physical beauty that you lose sight of her spiritual beauty."

Voluntary selflessness, which is the way someone has defined submission, is your secret weapon, dear Christian wife. By the silent preaching of a lovely life, you allow yourself to become a channel through which the Spirit of God can, and in His own time will, work in the life of your mate.

Several years ago *World Vision* magazine carried the story of a Hindu woman who had become a Christian. Because of her conversion she was subjected to a great deal of persecution by her husband. One day a missionary asked her, "When your husband is angry and persecutes you, what do you do?"

She replied, "Well, sir, I cook his food better; when he complains, I sweep the floor cleaner; and when he speaks unkindly, I answer him mildly. I try, sir, to show him that when I became a Christian I became a better wife and a better mother."[8]

I don't think The Principle of Submission as Strategy could be better stated. And according to *World Vision*, the husband, who could withstand all the public pulpit preaching of the missionary, could not withstand the private, practical preaching of his wife. Before long, he too gave his heart to Jesus.

Space does not permit me to say all that could or should be said about practical applications of this principle for Christian wives. Therefore, may I suggest, my sister, that you secure a copy of an excellent little book entitled, *Unequally Yoked Wives* by C. S. Lovett.[9] It describes, in greater detail than I could do in these few pages, some practical applications of this principle which God has honored as an evangelistic strategy to help wives win their unsaved mates. I don't agree with everything Lovett says, but he has much of real value to say. Like any strong medicine, his suggestions must be taken and used with care.

A Mind-Blower for Christian Men

With that word to women, let me make a few applications of this principle to Christian husbands who have unsaved wives or are married to gals who, instead of being filled with the Spirit, are living in a carnal state. In

essence, the application is the same for you as it is for your
Christian sisters. When Peter says, "You husbands,
likewise live with your wives in an understanding way [or,
as the King James has it, dwell with them according to
knowledge], as with the weaker sex, since she is a woman;
and grant her honor as a joint heir of the grace of life so
that your prayers may not be hindered" (I Peter 3:7), he is
saying: The best argument for Christianity is a Spirit-filled
Christian.

Don't try to manipulate your wife. Don't use your
maleness to coerce her into becoming a Christian. It won't
work! Instead, dwell with her "according to knowledge."
That is, discover her real needs and commit yourself to
meet them. Consider how Jesus would relate to her and do
the same. Don't assert your leadership; activate your headship. It is your responsibility as a Christian husband to be
like Jesus, the loving initiator of self-humbling service.

The following may come as a mind-blower to you, my
brother, but William Owen Carver, one of the greatest New
Testament scholars of this or any generation, has pointed
out that in all of the verses from Ephesians 5 which refer to
wives submitting to their husbands, the Greek verb
hupotasso is never in the imperative form.[10] *That is to say,
there are no God-given directives requiring wives to submit to their husbands! Their submission, as called for in
scripture, is always a voluntary adjustment on their part.
The imperative mood of this verb is never applied to the
wife! On the other hand, the standards set forth for
husbands in the same passages are reinforced by a series of
imperatives.*

Which is to say God places upon you, my Christian
brother, the very heavy responsibility of being head of
your wife. Not brain. Those functions in scripture are
associated with the word, heart. You are to be head in the
way Jesus is head. The source from which true, caring love
flows. Not ruler, but voluntary submitter. One who
presents his wife the all too rare gift of openness, vulner-

ability and loving support. One who initiates redemptive action. One from whom true care and ministry flow.

The emphasis throughout scripture is not upon your authority as husband, but upon your responsibility.

There is nothing in the Bible which allows you to demand obedience from your wife. You are not to say, "Be submissive, and then I'll love you." Instead, you are to be faithful to your responsibility to love her as Jesus loved His church. Look again at the graphic on our frontispiece. Do you see the cross penetrating the two wedding rings? That's how Jesus loved His church. He gave His life for it. And that's the love with which you are to love your wife: Calvary love!

In doing so, you are also to give her the freedom to decide to submit to you, even as Jesus gives you freedom to decide to submit to Him. Now, brother, that's love! And you won't be able to express it in the flesh. Jesus couldn't and didn't. His sacrificial love was possible because His flesh was filled and stayed full of the Holy Spirit. But the same Spirit who empowered the Lord Jesus can and will empower you if you ask Him to. That's a promise from the good Lord Himself. "If you then, being evil, know how to give good gifts to your children, how much more shall your Heavenly Father give the Holy Spirit to those who ask Him?" (Luke 11:13).

The word husband is a contraction of the phrase "house-band." A husband binds the house together. His band is love. Therefore, the single most important function you as a Christian husband have is to love your wife with Calvary love. As your wife becomes secure in such love, she will be free to respond happily and wholeheartedly.

Summing Up

To put it all together then, you, as a Christian husband, are under a God-given mandate to love your wife as Jesus loves His bride, the church. And you, my sister, as a Christian wife, are given the challenge of developing attitudes which encourage your man to be his best for God.

This chapter, because of the biblical passage upon which it is based, has had a more narrow purpose than the others in this book, for hopefully you are married to a Christian mate and both of you are eager for God's best. So, let's move back to our primary concern throughout this entire study: Biblical Principles for Christian Marriage.

Let me remind you again of the absolute necessity of a continuing commitment on the part of each of you to The Principle of Fullness Before Overflow. Just as a sailor locates his position at sea by shooting the sun or stars, so, too, you must constantly maintain your bearings by looking to God. You must put Him above everything and learn to see Him in everything. When you are wrong with Him everything else will be wrong. When you are right with Him, everything else will be right.

With His help, my Christian brother, you can become the loving initiator which is your high calling. With His help, my Christian sister, you can become the loving responder who, by your attitudes, encourages your man to reach for God's best. When that happens, each of you can freely and openly say with Roy Croft:

> *I love you,*
> *Not only for what you are,*
> *But for what I am*
> *When I am with you.*
>
> *I love you*
> *Not only for what*
> *You have made of yourself*
> *But for what*
> *You are making of me...*
>
> *I love you because you*
> *Are helping me to make*

Of the lumber of my life
Not a tavern
But a temple;
Out of my works
Of my every day
Not a reproach
But a song.

I love you
Because you have done
More than any creed
Could have done
To make me good.

You have done it
Without a touch,
Without a word,
Without a sign.
You have done it
By being yourself.[11]

10

The Principles of Fidelity and Forgiveness

"**If** . . . you are presenting your offering [gift] at the altar, and there remember that your brother has something against you, leave your offering there before the altar, and go your way, first be reconciled to your brother, and then come and present your offering. And if your brother sins, go and reprove him in private; if he listens to you, you have won your brother . . . Then Peter came and said to Him, 'Lord, how often shall my brother sin against me and I forgive him? Up to seven times?' Jesus said to him, 'I do not say to you, up to seven times, but up to seventy times seven' . . . When Jesus had finished these words, He departed from Galilee, and came into the region of Judea beyond the Jordan; and great multitudes followed Him, and He healed them there. And some Pharisees came to Him, testing Him, saying, 'Is it lawful for a man to divorce his wife for any cause at all?' And He answered and said, 'Have you not read, that He who created them from the beginning made them male and female, and said, "For this cause a man shall leave his father and mother, and shall cleave to his wife; and the two shall become one flesh"? Consequently they are no more two, but one flesh. What therefore God has joined together, let no man separate' " (Matthew 5:23,24; 18:15,21,22; 19:1-6).

While digging through my files I came across a story which aroused mixed emotions. It seems that while in seminary a young minister had been advised that should he forget the words of the marriage service he should quote Bible verses until he remembered. Sure enough, at his very first wedding, his memory failed and he started quoting verses. The first one which came to mind was, "Father, forgive them for they know not what they do!"

The reason that little story provoked mixed emotions is because, while his selection was quite humorous, it was also painfully appropriate. More than once I have looked across at a couple standing before me and wondered if they really understood the profound significance of the promises they were making to each other.

One time, just after his marriage ceremony, the young bridegroom said, "Is that all there is to it?"

"Not quite," I replied, "now all you have to do is live together for the rest of your lives."

This matter of living together—and doing so successfully—has been the concern of this book. We have discussed a number of biblical principles for Christian marriage, and I'm sure it must be obvious to you, as it is to me, that much more could be said. But I hope that by familiarizing you with these principles I have sufficiently whetted your appetite until now you are committed—you and your mate—to the marriage-long process of learning how to apply these principles to the various situations you will face.

In doing so, try to keep from getting hung up on the exceptions. The "what ifs" and "supposes." You and your mate have been learning a life-style for Christian marriage—a way of relating to each other which will enable the two of you to reach your full potential as marriage mates, thereby experiencing God's ideal for you as described in Genesis 1 and 2.

Obviously, there'll be times when this fallen world won't accommodate God's ideal. On those occasions, you may find yourself settling for a second-best solution to an emergency situation.

Handling Exceptions

Take the matter of decision-making. It's God's ideal that there be definite mutuality in that. The object is to reach a decision, not by using your power, but by negotiating a solution in which nobody wins at the expense of another person's losing. That takes time. Especially if children are involved. There are bound to be occasions when the clock works against you. Then, instead of being able to do the right thing, you may have to settle for doing the best thing under the circumstances. Mom or dad may have to simply exercise parental authority and say, "The answer is no."

"Why?"

"Because I said so. I'll explain my reasons later."

That sounds arbitrary. And it is! But if trust has been firmly established—if the spirit of mutuality has become the prevailing atmosphere in your Christian home—then such emergencies can be handled lovingly and effectively without rancor. The more preferable communicative process described in chapter eight can be bypassed, because everyone involved will understand that love is always the motive behind an arbitrary decision.

Awhile back, I received a letter from Ruth Harms Calkin, whose poems I quote from time to time. (If you want a delightful experience, I urge you to read her tiny book entitled, *Tell Me Again, Lord, I Forget*, published by David C. Cook, Elgin. It's a wonderful collection of prose-poetry which will bring you many blessings as it has Lucille and myself.) In her letter Ruth tells of spending a few days at a hotel in Palm Springs—a place she calls "my personal, spiritual Hawaii"—where she had gone to get the mental tangles untangled. Sitting on the edge of the pool one afternoon, quietly watching the happy splashers, she saw an attractive mother step to the edge of the pool and beckon to her young daughter. The child was about four, a lovely little thing, and on this occasion, at least, had a definite mind of her own. No way did she want to leave the pool.

"Please let me stay, Mother, please. I want to play with the kids. Please, Mother?"

Her mother was calm but insistent. "We must be in the room to meet Dad when he comes, Jennifer."

"You meet him. I know him already. Let me stay, Mother, please."

"Jennifer, the answer's no, just no. There isn't any life-guard on duty; the sign says I mustn't leave you here alone. Now, please don't ask again."

In a burst of exasperation and explosive tears, the little girl climbed out of the pool. "You don't like me, Mother, you really don't like me."

Her mother smiled as she hugged the quivering little frame close to her body and, with deep understanding, said, "Sometimes it feels that way, honey. I know it feels that way. But," she added as they walked off hand-in-hand, "isn't it good that our feelings don't always substantiate the facts? Because I really do like you, you know."

The little girl looked up, smiled and said, "Yes, Mother, I know."

That's just one illustration of an exception when there wasn't time to go through the whole communicative process to arrive at a no-lose situation. However, it is also an illustration, I think, of how arbitrary problem-solving can work effectively when everyone involved knows love is the motive in the making of the decision.

A Total Commitment

Marriage can be one of the best things that ever happens

to a person, or it can be the worst. Since no relationship is so satisfying and no experience so sublime as a truly Christian marriage, it just makes sense for you and your mate to master and apply the teachings of scripture on this subject. Among other things, you must come to grips with The Principles of Fidelity and Forgiveness.

Christian marriage is "a total commitment of the total person for total life. Anything less is not Christian marriage."[1] When Jesus said, "For this cause a man shall leave his father and mother, and shall cleave to his wife; and the two shall become one flesh; consequently they are no more two, but one flesh" (Matthew 19:5,6), He was making it clear that in God's ideal for your Christian marriage fidelity is assumed. However, it may come as a surprise to you to learn that genuine faithfulness goes far beyond genital fidelity. You may never engage in sexual activity outside marriage and yet fail to understand what it really means to be faithful.

The biblical Principle of Fidelity relates to your being one. Therefore, it involves what you do as well as what you don't do. In the biblical sense, as Andrew Greeley points out:

> Fidelity means the permanent, public, solemn and irrevocable commitment to dedicate [yourself] to bring out the best in both [your] partner and [yourself]. Infidelity is not the same as adultery, at least in its primary meaning. Infidelity means quitting, giving up on [your] relationship when there are still possibilities remaining.

He then goes on to make this thought-provoking statement:

> As long as there is a commitment to continue efforts to try to expand and to grow, to be a better, more generous and more effective lover, then adultery does not of itself destroy the primary fidelity of [a marriage]. It is an unfortunate and

ugly incident, but it does not necessarily revoke the primary commitment. Fidelity assumes that the basic evaluation of the other, which led to the original commitment, was a correct one; it may have been naive or incomplete, but it was commitment which saw something valuable and admirable in the other. Fidelity persists in believing that the original valuation was correct and that it would be a mistake to abandon without further effort the struggle to achieve the good things that the original commitment promised.[2]

Being faithful does not mean you lose the ability to feel strongly about someone other than your spouse. The capacity to form a new affection is always present. When one has lost a husband or wife (through death, for instance), he or she can, and many do, develop a deep and abiding love for a second life-partner.

But this ability to feel strongly about another person can be a curse, as well as a blessing. The tug of unexpected and unpredictable emotions can touch anyone. That's why our Lord gave such clear-cut instructions about guarding your thought life (Matthew 5:27-28).

Jesus was aware of the wholesome pleasure a man might feel in looking at a lovely woman, or the delight with which a woman might look upon an attractive man. He also knew there is nothing evil in that. It's a normal, natural, quite beautiful reflex action.

Your mouth may water at the sight of a perfectly broiled T-bone steak quite regardless of whether or not it's on your plate. Similarly, you may feel "that certain kind of feeling" upon meeting an appealing person of the opposite sex, even though that person doesn't belong to you. That isn't sinful. That's the way God made you. So you must keep in mind the difference between real guilt and false guilt. Real guilt has to do with what you *do* about that feeling.

Sometimes it's hard to tell the difference between the two. But one thing is absolutely certain: there is nothing sinful in the basic attraction between the sexes. However, Jesus understood human nature so well He knew that long before an open act of unfaithfulness occurs there is nearly always a period of secret disloyalty which prepares the way. Therefore, He set a standard of fidelity which begins in the area of your thoughts, not your actions. In this way you can protect yourself against temptations which, if given encouragement, might be more than you can handle.

True Freedom

Now, as you might expect, genital fidelity is really in your own best interest. Otherwise, the loving Heavenly Father would not have set marriage up that way. God is genuinely interested in your highest good, and fidelity is for people who insist upon getting the most out of sex, not the least.

There's a lot of propaganda these days in favor of "open marriages" and "free love." But open marriages are devoid of closeness and "free love" is really loose love.

As George E. Sweazey declares, "Loose love and genuinely free love are exact opposites. It is only in the lifelong loyalty to one person that love has a chance to explore the heights and depths and find its full expression. This is a freedom that is lost in the cramped bondage of compulsive sex."[3]

But that won't happen in your Christian marriage unless you and your mate are *un*willing to settle for a stale and static physical relationship. If that part of your life together is to provide you with the most instead of the least, the two of you must bring to it a spirit of sensitivity and adventure.

Married people feel great guilt if they have a transient affair outside of marriage. And they should! Unfortunately, however, they feel little or no guilt when they allow the physical relationship within marriage to become dull and routine. Has it ever occurred to you that, by celebrating your love in a faithful and fascinating way you and your mate are creating an atmosphere in your home which reveals God's love to the world?

Ponder this quote from Andrew Greeley:

It is to be presumed that most married couples do not view the art of sexual intercourse as a reflection of God's fidelity, for, after all, it occurs in the privacy of their bedroom with the door closed and the light dim. How could they possibly believe that improving their skills at bringing each other pleasure reflects God's implacable commitment to His people. They don't think of these things, in all likelihood, because nobody has ever suggested to them that the quality of their love—of which sexual intercourse is, of course, at the very center—is the most effective way they have of revealing God's love to the rest of the world.

To the extent that a man and a woman have settled for a static and dull genital relationship, they have settled for a marriage which is a very inadequate reflection of God's love for mankind. And to the extent that they are committed to improving the surprise and pleasure, the excitement, the challenge of what goes on between the sheets, they are reflecting God's commitment to His people.[4]

All of which is to say that fidelity is essentially a decision. A decision to settle down to the serious business of building your whole marriage into a relationship which is not only permanent and free from impurity, but alive and fulfilling in every possible way.

It's a formidable decision. A decision which you make by deliberate choice. A decision in which you say, as Andre-Maurois has put it, "I bind myself for life; I have chosen; from now on my aim will be, not to search for someone who

162

will please me, but to please the one I have chosen."[5]

Marriage and the Creating of Love

There is a dangerous fallacy afloat that if people fall in love, they should marry, and if they cease to be in love, they should divorce. But as George E. Sweazey points out:

Marriage is not the result of love, it is the opportunity for love. People marry so they may find out what love is. It is not destiny that makes a person the one true love, it is life. It is the hardships that have been faced together. It is bending over children's sickbeds and struggling with budgets; it is a thousand good-night kisses and good-morning smiles, it is vacations at the seashore and conversations in the dark; it is a growing reverence for each other which comes out of esteem and love.

George Sweazey continues:

The fallacy of the 'one and only' is mistaken only in that it is premature. Marriage is the union of two persons who are meant only for each other; but that is the result of marriage, not its precondition. A little clear logic makes us admit that the choice of a mate depends upon availability. When we are ready, we do the best we can within our range of acquaintance; then, happily, romantic love kindles and we marry with delight. Within the marriage real love begins.[6]

Through fidelity—that irrevocable commitment which refuses to give up on your relationship—you and your mate are able to build something between yourselves which is unique and irreplaceable. You *create* a love which spares you from the tragedy of comparing and second-guessing. Did I marry the right person? Could I have made a better catch? Does my spouse measure up to those of my friends?

Once a commitment has been made, the only appropriate questions are: Am I being the right mate? Am I becoming a better catch? Am I measuring up as a spouse in terms of being the loving initiator-responder my mate deserves and needs?

In the final analysis, marriage is not the result of love, it is the opportunity for love. It is the atmosphere in which true love has a chance to grow. The biblical Principle of Fidelity involves your total person. Genital fidelity only requires your body, but your mind can be a thousand miles away and your emotional switch turned off.

Biblical fidelity is something else again. It requires your full presence. Your sensing body. Your thinking mind. Your feeling heart. To be present in spirit is not adequate compensation to your mate when you are absent in body. He or she wants *all* of you there.

Similarly, to be present in body but absent in spirit is to deprive your life partner of your full presence. Therefore, fidelity, in the biblical sense—in the sense of your becoming one flesh—requires the totality of all you are: body, soul and spirit. It means you must be fully there.

I have stated this principle in several different ways because, if you're like most of us, you've been terribly concerned about genital infidelity. But it may never have occurred to you, as it had not to me until I pondered it deeply, that true fidelity means much more than not doing certain things. It was when I saw fidelity in the biblical sense that I began to realize how superficial my understanding of infidelity had been.

I became aware of my need to make a brand-new commitment to Lucille. A commitment to closeness. For without closeness fidelity is an empty word. It occurs to me that more Christians are in need of forgiveness on this score than we may realize.

The two principles—fidelity and forgiveness—fit so closely together, for when you fail each other, you are to

164

forgive each other, even as the Father forgives when you fail Him.

The Big Word in Christian Marriage

Aren't you glad the big word in Christian marriage isn't justice? It's love! Not halfway love. All-the-way love. One hundred and ten percent type love. A love which springs from knowledge and understanding. The reason God loves you is because He understands you. The reason He understands you is because He knows you (Psalm 139). This convinces me that if you really know your mate you'll understand what he or she does. More important, you'll understand why he or she does it.

Do you remember that beautiful prayer of St. Francis? "Lord, grant that I may seek more to understand than to be understood." Paul Tournier, the great Swiss Christian psychiatrist, feels so strongly about the need for understanding in the Christian marriage he says, "A husband and wife should become *preoccupied* with it—lost in it— engrossed to the fullest in learning what makes the other one tick, what the other one likes, dislikes, fears, worries about, dreams of, believes in, and *why* he or she feels that way."[7]

The Bible made the same recommendation many centuries ago. "Be kind to one another; be understanding. Be as ready to forgive others as God for Christ's sake has forgiven you" (Ephesians 4:32, J. B. Phillips). That's a text worth memorizing, or, better yet, worth placing in a conspicuous spot for all members of your family to see. For to know all is to understand. To understand all is to love. To love is to forgive.

Three Essential Steps to Forgiveness

When you think of the broader, biblical meaning of fidelity, it becomes clear that both partners usually have a share of the guilt of infidelity. If the mate who is innocent in the eyes of the law can take the first step by confessing his or her guilt and asking for forgiveness, it will help the other mate to be less defensive, admit his or her own guilt, and also seek forgiveness. This will require that you take the three essential steps to forgiveness: confession, repentance and cleansing.

You may need to approach your mate by saying something like this: "God has convicted me of..." and then mention a very specific thing. That's confession. "I'm truly sorry and want to change." That's repentance. Sometimes you may have a struggle at this point because, even as you are in the act of repentance, your mind is conjuring up thoughts about what it might be like to repeat the very thing you are repenting of. So you may need to move to another level of repentance in which you say, "I don't want to want to do what I've done. I want to want to change." Third, "Will you forgive me?" That's cleansing. And it's imperative that you include this third step in the process. It completes the cycle by bringing healing to the forgiver as well as the forgiven.

A Word of Caution

If you've been guilty of a serious breach of your marriage vows, may I caution you to resist the subtle temptation to use confession as the means of hurting your mate rather than bringing healing to him or her. Often it's better that you bare your soul to God alone—or to some trusted, *professional* counselor—than to ask your partner to hear you out when he or she may not have the ability to creatively handle what you say.

Dr. Louis Evans, Sr., tells of a young man who suddenly felt the need for a "confessional catharsis." During one of the world wars he had had relations with two French girls in Paris. He thought he should get this "off his chest." But, according to Dr. Evans, the wife was unable to accept the blow, and committed suicide by taking poison. "She was not spiritually capable of being a confidante," he explains. "A gushing, thoughtless confession can destroy rather than mend."[8]

Forgiveness and Self-Love

To be forgiving and to be forgiven calls for a healthy self-love. Some folk don't understand that. They get self-love and selfishness mixed up. They are not the same; they are opposites. Jesus commanded, "You shall love your neighbor as yourself" (Mark 12:31). He didn't say, "Love your neighbor *better* than yourself." Nor did He command, "Love your neighbor and *hate* yourself." Jesus said, "Love your neighbor *as* yourself."

What will happen if you take this command of Christ's seriously? For one thing, it will free you to accept God's forgiveness for yourself. For another, it will free you to extend your forgiveness to your mate. Refusing to forgive yourself when God has forgiven you is not a virtue; it is a sickness. Refusing to forgive others when God has done so is not a strength; it is a weakness. But a healthy self-love will help you overcome both hurdles. It will free you to forgive as you have been forgiven.

Forgiveness Is Something You Do

What is forgiveness? Perhaps you can best grasp the answer by discovering what forgiveness is not. Forgiveness is not forgetting. As a matter of fact, you're wired up in such a way that it's impossible to forget. Your brain is a physical computer with an awesome memory bank, so that, while you may forgive, it's not likely you'll ever forget. Your brain won't allow it. So forgiveness is not forgetting.

Forgiveness is not pretending. There is nothing to be gained by kidding yourself and acting as if what happened never happened. As David Augsburger says, "No amount of phony smiles and saccharine sweetness can turn the clock back. What is done is done. Forgiveness must accept the fact of the injurious act and reckon with it honestly."[9]

Forgiveness is not ignoring. It's not a charade in which you play the martyr and overlook what's been done. To say that is to say it doesn't matter when it does matter. It matters very much.

Forgiveness is not a feeling. It is not a balm that makes the hurt go away so you suddenly feel cuddly and warm inside. Not at all.

Forgiveness is not something you feel. It is something you do. It is deliberately deciding to let go of the hurt and let God bring the healing. Once you have done that, you will have extended forgiveness even though you may not feel like it.

Corrie ten Boom likens it to letting go of a bell rope.[10] If you've ever seen a country church with a bell in the steeple, you'll remember that to get the bell ringing you have to tug awhile. Once it's begun to ring, you merely maintain the momentum. As long as you keep pulling, the bell keeps ringing. Miss ten Boom says forgiveness is letting go of the rope. It's just that simple. But when you do so, the bell keeps ringing. Momentum is still at work. However, if you keep your hands off the rope, the bell will begin to slow and eventually stop.

It's like that with forgiveness. When you decide to forgive, the old feelings of unforgiveness may continue to assert themselves. After all, they have lots of momentum.

But if you affirm your decision to forgive, that unforgiving spirit will begin to slow and will eventually be still. *Forgiveness is not something you feel, it is something you do. It is letting go of the rope of retribution.*

One of the strongest statements on forgiveness as it relates to marriage is from the pen of David Augsburger:

> Forgiveness takes place when love accepts—deliberately—the hurts and abrasions of life and drops all charges against the other person. Forgiveness is accepting the other when both of you know he or she has done something quite unacceptable.
>
> Forgiveness is smiling silent love to your partner when the justifications for keeping an insult or injury alive are on the tip of your tongue, yet you swallow them. Not because you have to, to keep peace, but because you want to, to make peace.
>
> Forgiveness is not acceptance given 'on condition' that the other become acceptable. Forgiveness is given freely. Out of the keen awareness that the forgiver also has a need of constant forgiveness daily.
>
> Forgiveness exercises God's strength to love and receive the other person without any assurance of complete restitution and making of amends.
>
> Forgiveness is a relationship between equals who recognize their need of each other, share and share alike. Each needs the other's forgiveness. Each needs the other's acceptance. Each needs the other. And so, before God, each drops all charges, refuses all self-justification, and forgives. And forgives. Seventy times seven. As Jesus said.[11]

Let me share one of the times I saw this principle in action. There was a young man who was head-over-heels in love with a beautiful young girl to whom he became engaged. While he was away in the service, she got mixed up with another fellow who swept her off her feet and she became pregnant by him. She had sense enough to know she didn't love this other man. To marry him would only add insult to injury. Two wrongs would not make a right. However, she returned the engagement ring to the young man who was in the service and went into seclusion.

When her former fiance heard rumors of what had happened, he arranged through his chaplain for an emergency leave. Knowing I had helped her, he stopped by to see me. He wanted to find her. When I told him she was in a home for unwed mothers, he cried as if his heart would break. I don't think I've ever seen a young man weep as that lad wept that day. He wanted to see her, but she refused.

"Tell him," she told me, "I can only hope he'll forgive me and forget me. We must never meet again."

He persisted and finally she agreed to meet him. When they met in the drab parlor of that home, he took her in his arms, told her how much he loved her and that he would never, ever let her go as long as she lived.

At first, she was a bit wary. But when he said he wanted to marry her at once and make the unborn child his own, her defenses crumbled. With tears of joy bathing her cheeks, she consented. Arrangements were made for her to be released from the agreement to place the baby for adoption. The young man, out of his own funds, paid the home for the services they had rendered, and I had the joy of uniting them in marriage.

Today, if you were to meet them, you would affirm my judgment that they are more deeply in love than almost any couple I know. The devotion of that young wife to her husband is something unique. She loves much because she had been forgiven much. Forgiven, I think, as Jesus would forgive.

We began by saying, "This is not a typical 'how to'

book." By now you know that's true. You have not been given final answers to the numerous problems confronting those who would experience marriage at its best. However, the principles presented here were devised by our Lord to help you achieve that goal and they will work if you work them.

It is my prayer that, having caught a glimpse of Perfect Marriage—marriage as God wants yours to be—you and your mate will make a fresh commitment to Him and each other. A commitment to master these principles and be mastered by them, thus qualifying *your* marriage as truly Christian. Blessings!

Notes

1. The Principle of Fullness Before Overflow

1. Hannah Whithall Smith, *The Christian's Secret of a Happy Life* (Old Tappan, NJ; Fleming H. Revell Co., 1952), p. 106.

2. The Principle of What It's For

1. Helpful tool is The Marriage Expectation Inventory © 1976 Family Life Pub., Inc., Box 427, Saluda, N.C. 28773.

2. Leonard Zunin, *Contact: The First Four Minutes* (New York: Ballantine Books, 1972).

3. The Principle of Equality With Diversity

1. David W. Augsburger, *Cherishable: Love and Marriage* (Scottsdale, PA: Herald Press, 1971), p. 47.

2. Dwight Small, *Design for Christian Marriage* (Old Tappan, NJ: Fleming H. Revell Co., 1959), p. 34.

4. The Principle of Responsible Headship

1. John Stuart Mill, "The Subjection of Women" as reprinted in John Stuart Mill and Harriet Taylor Mill, *Essays on Sex Equality*, edited by Alice S. Rossi (Chicago: University of Chicago Press, 1970), pp. 235-36.

5. The Principle of Prevailing Atmosphere

1. "Spiritual Gifts Series" tapes. Order through Project Winsome Publishers, P.O. Box 111, Bakersfield, CA 93302.

6. The Principle of Diversity With Unity

1. Ogden Nash's poem, "The Oyster," printed in *Pith and Vinegar* edited by William Cole (New York: Simon & Schuster, 1969).

2. Donald and Inge Broverman, "Sex Role Stereotypes and Clinical Judgments of Mental Health," *Journal of Consulting and Clinical Psychology* 34 (1970:1-7). Published in summary form by Jo-Ann Gardner, *The Face Across the Breakfast Table* (Pittsburgh: Know, Inc., 1970).

3. *Alliance Witness,* May 31, 1961.

4. Quoted by Ray C. Stedman in a sermon entitled, "What Every Husband Should Know," p. 4.

7. The Principle of Sexuality

1. Pitirim A. Sorokin, "The Case Against Sex Freedom," *This Week* magazine, January, 1954, p. 7.

2. C. S. Lewis, *Christian Behavior* (New York: The Macmillan Company, 1943), p. 27.

3. George E. Sweazey, *In Holy Marriage* (New York: Harper & Row, 1966), p. 65.

4. Augsburger, *Cherishable: Love and Marriage,* p. 89.

5. David R. Mace, *Whom God Hath Joined* (Philadelphia: Westminster Press, 1953), p. 42.

6. Ibid, p. 42-43.

7. *The Christian Understanding of Sex* (Boston: Whittemore Association, Inc.) p. 6.

8. Sweazey, *In Holy Marriage*, p. 84.

9. Ibid, p. 84.

8. The Principle of Communication

1. Augsburger, *Cherishable: Love & Marriage*, p. 57.

2. We were first introduced to this concept at a Marriage Encounter weekend (Marriage Encounter, 295 Northern Boulevard, Great Neck, NY). Similar weekends are conducted by Christian Marriage Encounter, P.O. Box 1342, Colo. Springs, CO and Christian Marriage Communications, P.O. Box 155, Garden Grove, CA 92640.

3. From the title of a book by the same name published by Guidepost Associates, Pawling, NY.

9. The Principle of Submission as Strategy

1. William Barclay, *The Letters of James and Peter* (Philadelphia: The Westminster Press, 1958), p. 247.

2. Ibid, p. 258-59.

3. *Christopher News Notes*, No. 189 (12 East 48th St., New York, NY 10017).

4. Louis H. Evans, *Your Marriage—Duel or Duet?* (Old Tappan, NJ: Fleming H. Revell Co., 1962), p. 116-17.

5. John M. Drescher, "Why I Stopped Praying for My Family," *Eternity* magazine, (June, 1971), p. 9.

6. Barclay, *The Letters of James and Peter*, p. 259-60.

174

7. William L. Coleman, "Spousehold Hints...His...Hers," *Moody Monthly* (February, 1973), p. 47.

8. David R. Neibolas, "Foot Prints" *World Vision* magazine (January, 1966), p. 23.

9. C. S. Lovett, *Unequally Yoked Wives* (Baldwin Park, CA: Personal Christianity, 1968).

10. William Owen Carver, *The Glory of God in the Christian Calling* (Nashville: Broadman Press, 1949), pp. 168-69.

11. Attributed to Roy Croft, "Love," *Best Loved Poems of the American People,* compiled by Hazel Felleman (Garden City, NY: Doubleday, 1936), p. 25.

10. The Principles of Fidelity and Forgiveness

1. H. Norman Wright, *Communication: Key to Your Marriage* (Glendale, CA: Regal Books, 1974), p. 12.

2. Andrew Greeley, *Sexual Intimacy* (Chicago: Thomas Moore Press, 1973. Quoted in *Faith At Work* magazine, April 1974, pp. 8-9).

3. Sweazey, *In Holy Marriage,* p. 78.

4. Greeley, *Sexual Intimacy* (Quoted in *Faith At Work* magazine, p. 8).

5. David R. Mace, quoted in *Success in Marriage,* p. 124.

6. Sweazey, *In Holy Marriage,* pp. 29, 95.

7. Paul Tournier, *To Understand Each Other* (Atlanta: John Knox Press, 1962), p. 58.

8. Louis H. Evans, *Your Marriage—Duel or Duet* (Old Tappan, NJ: Fleming H. Revell Co., 1962), p. 99.

9. Augsburger, *Cherishable: Love and Marriage,* p. 143.

10. Corrie ten Boom, "I'm Still Learning to Forgive," *Guidepost Magazine,* (November, 1972), p. 5.

11. Augsburger, *Cherishable: Love and Marriage,* p. 146.

The material in this book is also available as a cassette album (ten cassettes with listening guides) through Project Winsome Publishers, P.O. 111, Bakersfield, CA 93302.